America:
Dark Slide

Bright Future

America:
DARK SLIDE

BRIGHT FUTURE

Dr. Judith Reisman *and*
Dr. Lloyd Stebbins

XULON PRESS

Xulon Press
2301 Lucien Way #415
Maitland, FL 32751
407.339.4217
www.xulonpress.com

© 2020 by Dr. Judith Reisman and Dr. Lloyd Stebbins

All rights reserved solely by the author. The author guarantees all contents are original and do not infringe upon the legal rights of any other person or work. No part of this book may be reproduced in any form without the permission of the author. The views expressed in this book are not necessarily those of the publisher.

Unless otherwise indicated, Scripture quotations taken from the King James Version (KJV) – *public domain*.

Scripture quotations taken from the Holy Bible, New International Version (NIV). Copyright © 1973, 1978, 1984, 2011 by Biblica, Inc.™. Used by permission. All rights reserved.

Scripture quotations taken from the New American Standard Bible (NASB). Copyright © 1960, 1962, 1963, 1968, 1971, 1972, 1973, 1975, 1977, 1995 by The Lockman Foundation. Used by permission. All rights reserved.

Printed in the United States of America.

ISBN-13: 978-1-6305-0791-6

WHY THIS BOOK? WHY NOW?

WHAT'S IN IT FOR YOU?

Our beloved American culture has been in decline since World War II. In recent decades, the decline accelerated. Today, the accelerating deterioration of America continues at a breathtaking speed. The ultimate end is chaos and some form of tyranny to control the chaos.

> ONLY GOD'S DIRECT INTERVENTION,
>
> THE GREATEST SPIRITUAL AWAKENING OF ALL TIME, OR
>
> THE MASSED EFFORTS OF LOVING, ENTHUSIASTIC, KNOWLEDGEABLE, AND VIRTUOUS
>
> JUDEO-CHRISTIAN BELIEVERS CAN SLOW AND REVERSE THE TERRIBLE TREND.

While studying 26 of the world's greatest civilizations for over 30 years, historian Arnold Toynbee, produced his magnum opus, a 12-volume, *Study of History*. He observed that, "<u>Civilizations die from suicide, not by murder</u>...So what does the universe look like?...It looks as if everything were on the move either toward its Creator or away from Him...The course of human history consists of a series of encounters...in which each man or woman or child... is challenged by God to make the free choice between doing God's will and refusing to do it. When Man refuses, he is free to make his refusal and to take the consequences."

The United States of America has been the hope of the world since the signing of the Declaration of Independence, July 4, 1776. That wonderful document in conjunction with the United States Constitution has until recently preserved and protected the greatest freedom since the Garden of Eden. Our spiritual and civil freedom is a gift of God and God alone. Throughout history there have always been individuals and groups who sought to maximize their own power and influence. Power can only be consolidated at the expense of individual freedom.

When power is concentrated, abuses increase in frequency and intensity unless there is an ironclad commitment to virtuous, moral, and ethical standards rooted in Judeo-Christian scripture. "We have no government armed with power capable of contending with human passions unbridled by morality and religion. Avarice, ambition, revenge, or gallantry, would break the strongest cords of our Constitution as a whale goes through a net. *Our Constitution was made only for a moral and religious people. It is wholly inadequate to the government of any other*." ***John Adams, Founder/President***

Until recent decades, there was a nationwide spiritual inertia that encouraged high standards throughout the American culture among believers and non-believers alike. Regretfully, throughout the last 50 years, there has been an accelerating drift away from God, the Bible and the cultural anchor of America's founding documents.

THE RELENTLESS MARCH TO AMERICA'S CIVILIZATIONAL SUICIDE MUST BE STOPPED FOR THE BENEFIT OF OUR CHILDREN AND GRANDCHILDREN AND ON TO POSTERITY, FOR THE BENEFIT OF THE WORLD.

What happened? The causes of America's precipitous decline are numerous. However, one, atheistic, pedophilic man, little-known today, had a far greater role in destroying America's culture than a mass of more famous people. His name: Dr. Alfred Kinsey famed, but much later proven fraudulent, "sexologist." Although his rise,

Why This Book? why Now?

public exaltation, and fall are profiled here, the same is discussed in far greater detail in Dr. Judith Reisman's other books.

The culturally devastating power and influence of one man was amplified and leveraged by his books, *Sexual Behavior in the Human Male*, later analog book on the human female, nationwide Kinsey lectures in packed university athletic stadiums, massive cash infusions by the Rockefeller Foundation, personal relationships with the most prominent American Civil Liberties Union (ACLU) attorneys, and direct assistance by the ACLU and Planned Parenthood. Kinsey's self-proclaimed "pamphleteer" Hugh Hefner enthusiastically broadcast Kinsey's message to the general public through the so-called "Playboy Philosophy," which packaged immorality in professional-sounding psychological euphemisms.

The Rockefeller Foundation proved to be a major driving force for developing the Model Penal Code (MPC) sponsored by the American Law Institute (ALI). All authors of the 1955 MPC were Kinsey partisans. The revolutionary ALI-MPC was accepted by the United States Supreme Court in *U.S. v Roth* (1957).

The Code bolstered by thousands of Kinsey's "expert" citations in hundreds of legal cases and many thousands of scholarly law journals, psychology journals, and sociology journals became the hammers to bludgeon from the law books at least 52 categories of sex and morality crimes, thus catastrophically undermining the Biblical foundation of the American culture.

Although Kinsey died in 1956 of his own sexual excesses, his message continues to be carried today with deafening loudspeaker intensity by the media, entertainment, and pornographic industries, as well as sports figures and politicians. The Kinsey Institute still exists and operates aggressively at Indiana University. The Institute and its progeny—including Planned Parenthood—continue to pump pornography, disguised as sex education materials, into the public school classrooms. Since the morally perverted propaganda has spilled over into classes other than sex-education, it has become virtually impossible for school children to avoid nearly total immersion.

Numerous nationally-known Christian leaders and Christian public service law firms have exerted Herculean efforts to right the legions of moral wrongs in the American culture. However, their astonishing, sometimes breathtaking, successes amount to playing legal "Whack-a-Mole" without the grassroots support of local churches and other places of worship.

THAT'S THE DARK SLIDE — WHAT'S THE BRIGHT FUTURE?

Judeo-Christian believers have been largely missing-in-action, virtually quarantined by the pressures of political correctness to within the four walls of their homes and four walls of their places of worship. No more! America is great, not because the people are great but because God is great. Like the ancient Israelites, God has blessed America as long as we have looked to Him as the source of everything. Similarly, His hand of blessing is removed to the extent that we "do what is right in our own eyes."

During one of the early low points of the American Revolutionary War, Thomas Paine wrote:

> These are the times the try men's souls. The summer soldier and the sunshine patriot (*weak or lapsed believers*) will, in this crisis, shrink from the service of his country (*and God*)…Tyranny (*Humanism*), like hell, is not easily conquered; yet we have this consolation with us that the harder the conflict, the more glorious the triumph. What we obtain too cheap, we esteem too lightly…Heaven knows how to put a price upon its goods; and it would be strange indeed if so celestial and article as <u>freedom</u> should not be highly rated…God Almighty will not give up a people to military

Why This Book? why Now?

(*or internal political*) destruction...who have so earnestly... sought to avoid the calamities of war...'Show your faith by your works,' that God may bless you...I thank God, that I fear not." **Thomas Paine**, Pennsylvania Journal, December 23, 1776 [*paranthetical application/emphasis added*].

In 1776, America faced external tyranny; today, we are experiencing a rapidly metastisizing internal political tyranny.

The "Bright Future" is that God has already given believers everything they need to overcome all obstacles. With the power of God's Spirit working through them, the raging torrant of national wrongs can be reduced to a lazy trickle. To do so, believers must clean their own house.

God commanded us to "...provoke them (*unbelievers*) to jealousy." [*Romans 11:11 KJV*] Most of us as individuals and as families have miserably failed that mission. We have eagerly sought the world's approval, following America's cultural decline, albeit a few steps behind—often while mouthing Biblical platitudes in religious groups. Even without using words our poor "witness" has trumpeted hypocrisy to outsiders.

Materialism paved the way to the emergence of masses of apathetic believers. Kinsey's powerful movement quickly filled the spiritual vacuum with waves of Humanism. Today, Judeo-Christian believers have become relegated from national leaders to worse than followers. To many powerful groups believers have become the enemy.

THE TARGET IS *YOU!* THE TARGET IS *YOUR FAMILY!*

BIG GUNS ARE AIMED AT YOUR FAMILY. WILL IT SURVIVE?

THE STUNNING HEAVY ARTILLERY AMASSED BY ANTI-FAMILY GROUPS IS FEARSOME.

The defense of your family is up to YOU! You must protect your family from cultural devastation and from government breaches of family sovereignty. However, you are not alone. God's power is still the greatest power in the universe and *it is readily available to believers*.

God's power and love are far stronger and longer lasting than any other. He is the *greatest defense* and the *greatest offense*.

The God-designed family is impregnable. It reflects the astonishing genius of our Creator. Did you know that in God's awesome family Dad and Mom are superheroes? Did you know that God's family child really is a miracle? Love truly conquers all. It begins with the family. Read about saturation love here.

To the extent that we restore unconditional love and strong families, demonstrate and broadcast unconditional love, we will create jealousy, rather than scorn, among unbelievers.

Our culture will metastisize love instead of conflict. Love will temper and in some cases overcome growing public tyranny. The ever-expanding influence will once again provide strong, compelling support for national Christian leaders and Christian public service law firms. The restored cultural stability will assure loving transmission of God's beautiful and perfect life-stabilizing message to future generations.

It is Up to YOU!

You can read this book and we hope and pray that you do. If you do so, be prepared to fully, irrevocably commit to restoring the joy and structure of God's biblical family as well as visibly restore and strengthen YOUR family and the families of your grown children, grandchildren, and on to posterity. Your family's light must shine brightly against the cultural background of darkness.

A powerful application of this book is its use for seminars sponsored by a church, groups of churches or other groups. Seminars may be lead by clergy, or local leaders. Upon request, the authors will be available to particpate. A study guide is also available.

The challenge is great; the goal is clear!

The greatest awakening of all time begins with YOU and ME.

Fueled by the Power of God's Wonderful Holy Spirit, Let's do it!

TABLE OF CONTENTS

WHY THIS BOOK? WHY NOW?

How a (Truly) Mad Scientist Secretly Took America from Purity to Promiscuity, from Devotion to Deviance

PART I:
KINSEY'S PERSONAL INFLUENCES

CHAPTER 1: KINSEY THE MAN 3
   Kinsey Biography 3
CHAPTER 2: THE KINSEY CONNECTIONS 9
   Kinsey Ties to Sexual Perversion 9
   Kinsey Ties to Criminals......................... 15
   Kinsey Ties to Darwin 17
   Kinsey Ties to German Nazis 18
   Kinsey Ties to Planned Parenthood 26
   Kinsey Ties to Eugenics and Leading Eugenicists 28

PART II:
POWERFUL LEVERAGE OF KINSEY'S LEGACY

CHAPTER 3: CULTURAL POWER 37
   Leverage by Big Money 37
   Leverage in American Law....................... 40
   Leverage in Politics 45

    Leverage in the Media 54

    Leverage by the Pornographic Industry 60

CHAPTER 4: ORGANIZATIONAL POWER 66

    Leverage by the Ongoing Kinsey Institute 66

    Leverage by Planned Parenthood 69

    Leverage by American Civil Liberties Union. 73

PART III: PATH TO RESTORATION

CHAPTER 5: WHERE ARE WE TODAY? WHAT COMES NEXT? 81

    The Power of Kinsey's Long-Term Impact. 81

    Where Were the Judeo-Christian Believers?. 83

CHAPTER 6: THE TARGET IS YOUR FAMILY 89

    Big Guns are Aimed at Your Family! Will It Survive?. . . . 89

    Powerful Anti-Family Enemies Aligned Against Your Family. 90

    Targets of the Anti-Family Groups Include Your Family . . .91

    Stunning Heavy Artillery Amassed by the Anti-Family Groups 92

    Fearsome Power Of The Anti-Family Groups 93

CHAPTER 7: FAMILY DEFENSE IS UP TO YOU 95

    You Must Protect Your Family From Cultural Devastation! 95

    Government Increasingly Breaches Family Sovereignty . . 96

Perpetual Tension Between the Sovereign Family and
the Sovereign Government 97

CHAPTER 8: GOD'S POWER IS THE GREATEST . . . 103

God's Power and Love are Far Stronger
and Longer Lasting Than Any Other 103

God is the Greatest Defense and the Greatest Offense . . . 108

CHAPTER 9: THE GOD-DESIGNED FAMILY IS IMPREGNABLE 114

Survival Skills For Your Family 115

The Genius of God's Family 116

Dad And Mom are Superheroes 118

God's Awesome Loving Family 122

The Miracle of God's Family Child 124

God Assigned To The Parents Primary Responsibility For
Children's Education. 125

The Pain When God's Family Turns Away From Him . . . 129

Leverage The Forgotten Power of The Homemaker 132

No Civilization Has Ever Survived The Breakdown of
The Family. 140

ABOUT THE AUTHORS 151

How a (Truly) Mad Scientist Secretly Took America from Purity to Promiscuity, from Devotion to Deviance

By Judith A. Reisman, Ph.D.

You might have heard the bit of folk wisdom that says if a farmer sees a turtle sitting on top of a fence post, he can be sure it did not get there by itself. My behind-the-scenes research into America's moral decline have confirmed the farmer's astuteness: this disaster did not just happen, it was planned. The sexual revolution was based on an academic fraud so breathtaking, on a hidden agenda so sinister, and on sex crimes so unspeakable, that I've devoted my life to exposing them and to undoing the devastation they caused.

The (truly) mad scientist who secretly spawned this revolution was Prof. Alfred Kinsey, pervert extraordinaire and author of the famous *Kinsey Reports* on human sexuality of 1948 and 1953. Crammed with shocking statistics, these purportedly "scientific" volumes seemed to prove that most Americans were committing immoral, perverted and even illegal sex acts on a regular basis. Later, Prof. Kinsey and his fellow revolutionaries would inaugurate the stealth fields of "sexology" and "sex education," using their alleged "scientific findings" to overthrow Judeo-Christian sexual morality and millennia of human experience.

Actress Laura Linney played Mrs. Kinsey in Fox's feature film "Kinsey," which starred Liam Neeson as Prof. Kinsey. In 2004 Linney accurately said, *"Any sort of sexual education that anybody has had in the past 50 years came right from the [Kinsey] Institute... So his impact is enormous, and in ways that it's probably impossible for us to completely grasp... When Kinsey published that*

America: Dark Slide-Bright Future

information, he changed our culture completely." (ABC News's "Primetime Live" show, "Kinsey," October 14, 2004.)

You and your loved ones are now living in the "post-Kinsey era" that was launched in 1948. Every hour of every day, you are affected by radically sexualized education, laws, healthcare, politics, media, entertainment, fashions and behavior, all institutionalized by Prof. Kinsey's disciples. If you are like most Americans, you probably wonder how we went from the America that the Greatest Generation knew to a place where...

- God and the Ten Commandments are purged from our public schools
- The Commandments were soon replaced on schoolhouse walls by STD and AIDS posters
- Doctors and major pharmaceutical companies criminally experiment on infants[1]
- "Assisted suicide" and euthanasia threaten the lives of sick and elderly people
- Countless Web sites make obscene pornography instantly available to all
- So many adults and youths are addicted to pornography that treating them is now a growth industry for sex therapists
- 65 million Americans have at least one venereal disease (now euphemized as "STDs")
- 19 million are infected each year with STDs, many incurable and some fatal
- Increasing numbers of university presidents, administrators, professors, coaches, doctors, clergy, teachers and school counselors have been convicted of obscene child pornography, torture and sex crimes against children
- Respected universities sponsor courses for credit in which vulnerable students "study" pornographic/obscene films

Why This Book? why Now?

- Sexually deviant professors require terrified students to view obscenity/pornography and to report their states of "arousal"
- More than 2,000 Pentagon personnel who paid for online child pornography/obscenity remain uninvestigated by authorities
- A famous Johns Hopkins University psychiatrist, Dr. Fred Berlin, "destigmatizes" pedophiles as mere "minor-attracted persons"
- Pedophiles seek to end age-of-consent laws—which they euphemize as "intergenerational male intimacy"
- Smiling politicians march in "gay pride" parades alongside the "North American Man-Boy Love Association"
- Homosexuals who arrange to couple together legally adopt children
- Police officers do nothing as nude men and women commit illegal perverted sex acts at public "gay" events
- Violating the will of the voters, judges and lawmakers impose homosexual "marriage" on entire states
- United Nations sex radicals pressure abortion "rights," "gay rights" and children's "sexual rights" on the entire world
- Abortionists killed more than 50 million unborn babies, creating a lucrative traffic in these babies' body parts
- Philanthropic foundations like Ford and Rockefeller, and scores of corporations like PepsiCo, Sears Roebuck, J.C. Penny, Office Depot, Barnes & Noble, Safeway, Target, Office Max, Home Depot, Costco, Walgreens, Hallmark Cards and Google, pour millions into marketing "gay," "transgender," bisexual, homosexual, etc., "rights"[2]
- In 2003, 60% of American Academy of Matrimonial Lawyers reported pornography induced divorce[3]
- Rapes and rape-murders of women and children, often serial in nature, are increasingly common occurrences

America: Dark Slide-Bright Future

- The careers of one politician after another implode in sex scandals involving adultery, even child abuse
- Movies and TV shows insert hetero and homosexual nudity, sex, rapes, gutter language and ridicule of sexual morality
- Major hotel chains make barely legal "teen" pornography and other obscene videos available to all their guests, of any age
- "Sexology" institutes train many thousands of "sexperts" and "sex educators" who impart anything-goes sex training to countless couples, educators, college students and schoolchildren
- Millions of children are force-fed transgender, heterosexual and homosexual sex "ed" assertions that children are "born that way"
- Classics such as *Tom Sawyer* are forgotten as publishers market award-winning "kiddie-lit" pornography featuring rape, incest, sodomy, homosexuality, transgender, suicide, masturbation and family nudity
- Schoolgirls increasingly think it harmless to post naked photos of themselves on the Internet or "sexting" them to current boyfriends
- The "news" media censor evidence that male and female teachers commit more child sex abuse than do priests and other clergy
- As was done earlier to American Indian and Australian Aborigine children, "over one million North American" children (circa 2002), ripped from innocent parents, are sent to shelters, jails and "foster" homes by "social workers" and judges[4]
- Both child and woman "sex trafficking" is a massive and growing industry in the USA and globally

Why This Book? why Now?

- The State markets "same-sex marriage" as normal, thus covers up early sex abuse as largely causal in bi/homosexuality/transgenders
- Legalizing "same-sex marriage" equates injurious, formerly criminal sodomy with the God-ordained conjugal act designed to cement the institution of matrimony for the dedicated rearing of children
- Over half of all children birthed by American women under 30 are born out of wedlock[5]
- In 1950, 96 percent of children overall had married parents; now 63 percent have married parents (resulting in 1.5 million fatherless children born each year)[6]
- In 1950, 85 percent of black children had married parents; now 35 percent have married parents[7]
- Fatherlessness costs $99 billion a year for basic care, plus homeless, criminal, rapist, suicidal, etc., youth[8]
- We have gone from two major venereal diseases in the 1960s to now having over 25, some incurable, even fatal[9]
- Thousands of pulpits remain silent about these horrors, and some religious leaders even condone them

These are just a few of the "bleeding indicators" of modern society's systemic sex sickness. I am sure you could add a few of your own. Yet irrational, cowardly, in-denial people will tell you that Americans have always done these things, and that today we are just more honest about reporting "normal" sexual conduct.

After you read this book, you will confirm that what you always knew in the deepest recesses of your mind, heart and soul is really true. You will also understand why, despite decades of financial, verbal and physical harassment, the Boy Scouts of America until very recently denied admission of homosexual leaders or scouts who say they are "gay."[10]

America: Dark Slide-Bright Future

Stolen Honor, Stolen Innocence, Stolen Family, Stolen America will prove to you the obvious: that what you perceive around you is not "just better reporting," but a deliberate destruction of our God-given right to normal, loving, conjugal living, and to living civilly and honorably, with a noble, healthy and sober character.

You will discover how a cadre of sexual psychopaths, like Kinsey, deliberately, deviously and deceitfully stole our national honor, as well as our children's and our own right to innocence, and to our historic, common-sense values of virtue in sex and in life. You will learn about our virtuous laws that had raised the age of consent to 16, 18 and even 21, had outlawed seduction, abortion, pornography, sodomy, adultery, etc., and often provided death or life in prison for rape—and <u>how these laws, in the post-Kinsey era, were systematically dismantled</u> by a cult whose malicious leader's own twisted sexuality drove him to assault the sexual morals and laws that had long protected and prospered our Judeo-Christian nation.

In the earlier books, I (The first person throughout this introduction is Dr. Judith A. Reisman.) introduced myself at length so that you, kind reader, would know something about my life and about how I came to discover Prof. Kinsey's sex crimes against children, his falsified data on Americans' sex lives and his deviant design to corrupt the "faithful city"—the United States. I will not do that this time, but let me tell you about one horrific incident that changed my life forever.

Why This Book? why Now?

I lived a very happy life until 1966, when my 10-year-old daughter (pictured at a much younger age on the right, with her mother) was raped by a 13-year-old friend of the family. She had told him to stop, but he persisted. She would like it, he said; he learned this from his father's *Playboy* magazines. The boy left the country before we learned of his crime, and the fact that my daughter was just one of several neighborhood children he had raped, including his own little brother. My heart broke for all the families involved. This appalling atrocity, I would later learn, fit a pattern that was typical among juvenile sex offenders. Over the years, that pattern would spread throughout society; it was an infectious environmental disease.

I might never have known about my daughter's victimization if she had not slipped into a deep depression. Only after I promised not to call the police would she talk about what happened. After assuring her it was not her fault, I called my dependable, staid aunt who listened sympathetically and who then declared, "Well, Judy,

America: Dark Slide-Bright Future

she may have been looking for this herself. Children are sexual from birth." Stunned, I replied that my child was *not* seeking sex.

Next, I dialed my Berkeley school chum, Carole, still seeking confirmation of my righteous fury at my daughter's violation, which I badly needed to hear. Instead, Carole counseled, "Well, Judy, she may have been looking for this herself. You know, children are sexual from birth." I wondered why I was hearing this same locution from two such different people who were so widely separated geographically. I did not realize I had just entered the world according to Kinsey. I would hear that "children are sexual from birth" again, but at that later date, I would learn the covered-up truth about its source.

Years after my daughter's trauma, following the trail of Prof. Kinsey's crimes led me to become involved with international scholarly conferences, federally funded investigations, the FBI, the Pentagon's Joint Chiefs of Staff and national and international governmental hearings on science fraud, sexual abuse and trafficking of children, juvenile delinquency, rape and other sex crimes, pornography, drugs, abortion and the other critical social and moral issues of our time. You can now find this information on my Web site, www.DrJudithReisman.com.

For now, let us fast-forward to 1976. Based on my professional writing and work in public television, at NBC, at ABC, on CBS's "Captain Kangaroo" show, and at a score of art and history museums, Case Western University admitted me, pending a 4.0 grade average. After I received my doctorate in Communications in 1977, I did a research report on children, women and pornography that was accepted by the British Psychological Association's International Conference on "Love and Attraction" at Swansea University, Wales. As I was leaving London for Wales, news headlines announced that the leader of the "Pedophile Information Exchange" (PIE), Tom

Why This Book? why Now?

O'Carroll, was touring the UK en route to promoting pedophilia at the Swansea conference. PIE listed sites and addresses where pedophiles could seduce and rape vulnerable children. But when Swansea University's housekeeping staff learned that O'Carroll was to speak on their campus, they went on strike. If he speaks, they declared, we'll walk—he won't promote sex with *our* children!

Earlier, I had clashed with a Tufts University professor, Larry Constantine, a *Penthouse* magazine board member who endorsed child pornography and pedophilia in his paper on "The Sexual Rights of Children." At an emergency meeting of the conference's speakers, he urged the international attendees to sign his "free speech" petition that insisted the strikers work and O'Carroll speak. I argued that as guests of Swansea, we had no right to threaten the staff and leave behind a community traumatized by a university-sponsored advocate of child molestation. I was the only speaker who did not sign Constantine's petition. Eventually the president of the university ruled that O'Carroll was not credentialed to speak, and housekeeping services resumed.

Why, I wondered, would academics support an advocate of child abuse, while the university's workers aggressively protected their children? I thought this showed callous contempt for the housekeeping staff's concerns about protecting children, and it increased my disappointment with the morality and integrity of the university community at large.

After O'Carroll fled the Swansea conference, I presented 80 slides depicting child pornography in *Playboy* magazine (and some in *Penthouse*). Later, as I left for London, a Canadian psychologist whispered to me that I was right, that images of child abuse in *Playboy* and *Penthouse* would trigger copycat sex crimes against children. But, he said, if I wanted to learn where *Playboy* publisher Hugh Hefner and this sexual abuse of children were stemming from,

America: Dark Slide-Bright Future

I should read about Prof. Alfred Kinsey in Edward Brecher's book, *The Sex Researchers*. "Why?" I asked. "I worked with Kinsey and Pomeroy," he answered. "One is a pedophile and the other a homosexual." Which is which, I asked? "Read and discover," he replied.

Flying back to the States, I realized I had just been witness to a growing, international, academic pedophile movement—people who were dependent on pornography, even at the conference, and who now sought sex with children. I had stumbled right into their midst. What kind of academic training, I wondered, was producing such a degraded and predatory intelligentsia?

Reading *The Sex Researchers*, I could not decide which was worse— the depictions of Prof. Kinsey's cold, criminal, experimental sexual abuse of infants and toddlers at The Kinsey Institute at Indiana University, or Brecher's eager celebration of Prof. Kinsey's methods of studying "child sex." This was madness! Incredulous, I checked Prof. Kinsey's book to verify Brecher's quotes. Yes! Brecher quoted Prof. Kinsey accurately—infants were genitally "tested" for their ability to have what he called orgasms, as were hundreds of other children. Prof. Kinsey was the world's "scientific" authority on "child sexuality."

After graduation from Case Western, doctorate in hand, I left America with my family to do research in Israel. In 1981 I sat in my mountaintop office at Haifa University, staring at Prof. Kinsey's world-famous book, *Sexual Behavior in the Human Male*. I was re-reading page 180, which contained something called Table 34. Had I missed or misunderstood something? I had read biographies of Prof. Kinsey, hundreds of positive articles and chapters about him and his work, and the few scathing reviews, but nowhere had anyone mentioned these tables and graphs of "child orgasms." <u>*The thousands of international scientists who quoted and cited Prof. Kinsey were blind to what he put right before their eyes*</u>.

Why This Book? why Now?

After Prof. Kinsey's death in 1956, Paul Gebhard his co-author succeeded him as director of The Kinsey Institute. In February, 1981, I wrote to the Institute, asking several questions, including where they got their child orgasm data for Tables 30-34. On March 11, 1981, Gebhard stunned me when he replied, saying the child orgasm figures came from "parents...nursery school owners or teachers... homosexual males," some of whom used "manual or oral techniques" to record the number of alleged "orgasms" that infants and other children had while being timed with stopwatches by adults.

Four months later, on July 23, 1981, my paper, *"The Scientist As a Contributing Agent to Child Sexual Abuse; a Preliminary Consideration of Possible Ethics Violations,"* spotlighted Prof. Kinsey in the Abstracts of the Fifth World Congress of Sexology in Jerusalem. It was no surprise that my talk was standing room only. "Human sexuality" leaders from around the world attended: England, the USA, France, Denmark, Israel, Norway, Canada, Scotland, the Netherlands, Sweden and scores of other nations were represented by their top sex researchers, curriculum writers, therapists, counselors, etc. The entire conference was abuzz. Attendance at my talk on Prof. Kinsey was bigger than the one by Xaviera Hollander ("the Happy Hooker") on "Out of Touch with Sex."

Armed with Gebhard's confessions, I projected slides of Tables 30-34 and pages 160 and 161, including Prof. Kinsey's rates and speeds of "orgasms" of at least 317 infants and children (the youngest being two months old). I quoted his statement that many of a group of 196 children and infants "fainted," "screamed," "wept" and "convulsed!" Though he said these reactions represented sexual pleasure, I said, "No, this was evidence of children's terror and pain, and it was criminal." Only a sadomasochistic pedophile, I thought to myself, would call a child's convulsions "pleasure." The revered Prof. Kinsey was a sexual psychopath. The infamous Table

America: Dark Slide-Bright Future

34 is shown here. The others are available in Dr. Judith Resiman's book, *Stolen Honor Stolen Innocence: How America was Betrayed by the Lies and Sexual Crimes of a Mad "Scientist."*

AGE	NO. OF ORGASMS	TIME INVOLVED	AGE	NO. OF ORGASMS	TIME INVOLVED
5 mon.	3	?	11 yr.	11	1 hr.
11 mon.	10	1 hr.	11 yr.	19	1 hr.
11 mon.	14	38 min.	12 yr.	7	3 hr.
2 yr.	{ 7 / 11 }	9 min. / 65 min.	12 yr.	{ 3 / 9 }	3 min. / 2 hr.
2½ yr.	4	2 min.	12 yr.	12	2 hr.
4 yr.	6	5 min.	12 yr.	15	1 hr.
4 yr.	17	10 hr.	13 yr.	7	24 min.
4 yr.	26	24 hr.	13 yr.	8	2¼ hr.
7 yr.	7	3 hr.	13 yr.	9	8 hr.
8 yr.	8	2 hr.		{ 3	70 sec.
9 yr.	7	68 min.	13 yr.	{ 11	8 hr.
10 yr.	9	52 min.		26	24 hr.
10 yr.	14	24 hr.	14 yr.	11	4 hr.

Table 34. Examples of multiple orgasm in pre-adolescent males
Some instances of higher frequencies.

The crowd was silent. No questions. No challenges. Black silence. Finally, a tall, blond Nordic type who had been standing near the podium stepped forward and barked:

> I am a Swedish reporter, and I never have spoken out at a conference. That is not my role. But what is the matter with all of you? This woman has just dropped an atomic bomb in this very room, and you have nothing to ask? Nothing to say?

Hands shot up. The Kinsey Institute's chief librarian stood and said, "Let's have tea. This is not true." I simply quoted pages in Prof. Kinsey's own book and pointed to plainly visible tables of child torture. My angry moderator shut down the debate, but many

Why This Book? why Now?

people tacitly agreed an investigation was needed. Later, Sweden's director of sex education told me she was shocked that children were used without consent. However, *with* consent, she assured me, children could be sexually stimulated by adults, even parents—for their own good, of course. Late that afternoon my young Haifa University assistant, visibly shaken, joined me. She had just dined with the leaders of the international conference. My lecture was hotly condemned. Her 12 dinner companions all agreed that children could take part in "loving" (not angry) sex with adults.

It turned out that <u>*millions of dollars in grants* that such "experts" received for sex "education," research and "therapy," and even future profits in sex, drugs, films, "toys," etc., hinged on Prof. Kinsey's human sexuality "data."</u> (Millions of dollars still do, with more than $20 million in "health" grants showered on Kinsey Institute researchers alone just from 1986 to today.[11]) At this conference, I had just proven that the world's "sexperts" were following a child molesting, psychopathic, pornography-addicted, criminal con man. Little did I know then, that with the funding and reputations of universities and agencies worldwide riding on Prof. Kinsey's data, no investigation could—or would—ever be allowed.

But then things seemed to change. In 1982, not long after my exposé in Jerusalem of Prof. Kinsey's frauds, the U.S. Department of Justice's Office of Juvenile Justice and Delinquency Prevention (OJJDP) flew me back from Israel. I received an appointment as a Full Research Professor at American University (AU), to serve as the principal investigator for an $800,000 grant to investigate Prof. Kinsey's role in sex crimes against children and his link to images of children in mainstream pornography—specifically, *Playboy*, *Penthouse* and *Hustler* magazines.

The commercial sex industry, however, soon joined The Kinsey Institute and academic sexologists to keep Prof. Kinsey's crimes hidden. Years later I obtained copies of classified letters and packages secretly sent worldwide by The Kinsey Institute to discredit my findings about Prof. Kinsey and about child exploitation in *Playboy*, *Penthouse* and *Hustler*. As soon as the news media revealed my appointment at AU, The Kinsey Institute threatened to sue the school if I studied Prof. Kinsey, and it helped launch the first attempt in the U.S. Congress to kill my study. Violating both academic freedom and the public's right to know, AU killed my investigation of Prof. Kinsey—but it "allowed" me to continue researching child sexploitation in pornography.

Ever since 1984, The Kinsey Institute and its pro-pornography co-conspirators have maintained a constant vigil, lobbying legislators to suppress my findings and to hide the truth from the news media, professional conferences, journals, book publishers, etc.

My key opponents knew my researchers would find child sexploitation to be a raging, systemic theme in *Playboy*, et al., as well as finding advocacy of other crimes—e.g., gang rape of women and girls, seducing and then abandoning the women whom men impregnate, voyeurism ("peeping"), exhibitionism (exposing oneself), adultery, using prostituted women and girls, harming women who refused sex, etc. So Sen. Arlen Specter (then a Republican, now a Democrat) was chosen to lead two of three (yes *three*) congressional hearings to bushwhack my study. Failing that, he and his team would discredit me and the data in a news media barrage before we released our study.

Hence, my Department of Justice grant, signed in February, 1984, was followed by a major congressional investigation on April 11, 1984, led by Congressman Ike Andrews (D-NC) aide, Gordon Raley, who later wrote for *Penthouse* magazine. After this failed to kill the work, the Senate picked up the "no credibility" line for a hearing of its own on May 7, 1985, and yet another one on August 1, 1985.

Why This Book? why Now?

The national news media were lined up to report that our investigation of sexual abuse of children in mainstream pornography was a worthless boondoggle, and its investigator was equally worthless. My three key accusers were Sen. Ted (Chappaquiddick) Kennedy and two other senators, Senator Arlen Specter and Senator Howard Metzenbaum, who carefully hid their own conflicts of interest. Years later, the *Washington Times* (March 18, 1992) reported that Specter was funded by a pornography profiteer. We also turned up an awkwardly glowing *Penthouse* interview with Sen. Howard Metzenbaum in November, 1982.

On August 1, 1984, I testified before the Senate committee that "present in the content of all three magazines is a documentable evolution of children portrayed as viable sex targets." Portrayals of children, I noted, became "more sexually explicit and more violent over time." Obviously, Metzenbaum and the other senators didn't want the public to know that.

In November 1985, although my study was not yet complete, AU administrators locked me out of my files, refused to give me copies of my computer disks, held my report "in editing" for nearly two years (more on that in another book). Then, while denying me a copy, AU sent my "edited" report to OJJDP. Things became clearer when, during the AU "editing process," the chairman of AU's department of psychology, Dr. Elliot McGinnies, a key foe of my child pornography research was arrested for sex crimes against a child in his trailer at a nudist colony (*Washington Post*, September 19, 1986). He recently was rearrested. In 1990 AU president, Dr. Richard Berendzen, with unspeakable child pornography magazines tucked away in his presidential desk, was arrested for child sex-related offenses (*Washington Post*, September 23, 1990). The reasons for AU's efforts to stop my investigation of child sex abuse in mainstream pornography were glaringly obvious, even to the most naïve observer.

America: Dark Slide-Bright Future

The plot thickens. In November 1985 I was forced to leave my completed research with AU for "editing." I had no idea that AU would deliberately bowdlerize my two-year study and send their bogus document to OJJDP on September 2, 1986. Regrettably, I possessed only one original hard copy to compare to the AU brutally gutted document. What to do? After spending almost a year to find and correct the frauds, reenter the missing data and get approvals for the final work from my academic peers, I received an offer from Heaven, as it were. Dr. Jerry Falwell, founder of Liberty University, had somehow heard of my plight. He flew me to Lynchburg, Virginia, and provided a hotel, meals and his entire secretarial and publishing facility to reconstruct my 2,500 pages of research, stipulating only that his aid be anonymous. I agreed.

Three weeks later, my report was re-typed and all the graphs, charts and statistics were being re-entered when I received a curt, gratuitous deadline from OJJDP to deliver my corrected, complete report tomorrow or they would announce the rejection of my study. The next day! When Dr. Falwell learned of this sudden mandated OJJDP zero hour he organized an assembly line of kind ladies who stoically worked through the night, printing and collating the documents by hand. Six copies of each three-hole punched, quasi-leather-bound report in three-parts were ready in the morning. Charlie Judd, then executive director of Liberty Federation and Moral Majority accompanied me on the Falwell jet as we spun off to Washington, D.C. A taxi waited at the National airport to drive us to the OJJDP office. November 1986, Mr. Judd and I delivered multiple copies of my tome, on deadline, to a very sour faced and upset Robert Speirs, the OJJDP Administrator, and his even more peeved program monitor, Ms. Pamela Swain! We were unaware that as Mr. Judd and I left the unhappy couple, Speirs and Swain were busy couriering the peer-approved study out of their building

Why This Book? why Now?

in order to reject its' scientific findings. In another book, I will go into what happened after that—indeed, the battle had just begun.[12]

It was June 1, 1988 when I arrived again in Lynchburg for a TV interview with Dr. Falwell on the "Pastor's Study." After going into detail about what our research uncovered, Dr. Falwell smiled at me and said, in his easy, friendly voice...

DR. FALWELL: You did this for the Department of Justice. It was delivered to the Department of Justice, and I will assume that the wonderful Department of Justice would, by now, have done something wonderful about it.

DR. REISMAN: Well, that's what I would have assumed...but first of all, they blocked the publication of the report consistently. They claimed our academic peers didn't approve it. We proved that the academic peers did approve it. All of their statements and critiques were included, so that we thought that problem was solved. Just recently, this last month, a memo went out...

DR. FALWELL: I have it. Let me read this memo. It is unbelievable! It's on the screen there, but I'm going to read it to you. It was a memo distributed to the various divisional managers in the Justice Department responsible for reviewing this study. "Please be advised that I have received a memo from Charles A. Lauer, General Counsel, regarding the report 'Images of Children, Crime and Violence in Playboy, Penthouse and Hustler Magazines, Executive Summary' that was recently received in the office." That's your study. "Please review the following relevant portions of the memo from the office of General Counsel and notify all of your staff immediately." Then there is a writing of the law that says this is all illegal stuff and here's the bottom line, the last paragraph, "Please advise all staff that this report should not be duplicated or sent through the mails" because the law says "to print or distribute this is a crime." Now if it's a crime for the Justice Department managers to distribute this, why is it not a crime for Guccione, Hefner, and Flynt to distribute this?

DR. REISMAN: That's a very good question. Because they are referring specifically to the fact that we found child pornography, young people, under the age of 18...

DR. FALWELL: [Speaking about then-Attorney General Ed Meese] It would seem like there are forces beneath him that are very powerful.

DR. REISMAN: Very powerful. Incredibly powerful. Because what we see here is a federal report that identifies child pornography, and its researcher, identified as having done something illegal, while those who produce the material, make the profit on the material, continue to do what they've been doing and are not prosecuted. Playboy, Penthouse, these people are not prosecuted.

DR. FALWELL: Why would the Justice Department be attempting to squelch this report and refusing to act upon it?

DR. REISMAN: Well, it is my opinion that there is a very strong, a very powerful, sex-industry lobby that is having its way in the Department of Justice.

Indeed, after years of defamation of my work (and me), a new head of the OJJDP, Robert Sweet, investigated the whole shameful, dirty business and wrote, *"While the massive, affluent sex industry has employed nearly every technique in their arsenal, short of violence, to stop Dr. Reisman's work, they have not shown her* findings *to be incorrect or methodologically* flawed—*in even the smallest detail"* (August 25, 1994).

Why This Book? why Now?

And, as I have documented in *Stolen Honor, Stolen Innocence*, Kinsey's "pamphleteer," Hugh Hefner, had joined forces with The Kinsey Institute to threaten anyone who would let me investigate Prof. Kinsey.

In 1990, my first book, *Kinsey, Sex and Fraud* was released by a small Christian publisher, and in 1991, the same publisher released my book *"Soft" Porn Plays Hardball*. Phil Donahue, a popular TV talk-show host and Kinsey disciple, thinking to expose my work as bogus, put me on his show—and assessed Kinsey's worldwide importance:

> "Kinsey was to sexuality what Freud was to psychiatry, what Madame Curie was to radiation, what Einstein was to physics. Comes along this woman [Reisman] saying, 'Holy cow! E doesn't equal mc². *We've based an entire generation of education of sexologists on Kinsey, and Kinsey was a dirty old man.*'"

I agreed, but Donahue argued forcefully that Kinsey was really a conservative family man, a myth now fully disproven by his own laudatory biographers. The public has a right to know what has been covered up, and why. The nation has a responsibility to know *what happened to the children of Table 34* and how a demonic, Faustian sexual psychopath sold all of us his deviant, demented sexual revolution via colossal lies and trickery.

It is time to connect Prof. Kinsey, the father of the sexual revolution, sexology and "sex education," to the massive, growing, global addiction to pornography. Since 1948, public health report data have confirmed the staggering social costs and consequences of this sea change in the way America and the rest of the Western world have come to view human sexuality. As America's founding moral order has been jettisoned and the standard of judgment has shifted radically over the last 50 years, the statistical evidence proves that our country's present direction deserves review, and on an urgent basis. The crisis is far worse and more menacing to our children and our nation's survival than even Mr. Donahue said. *For what will become of a society that has based three "generations of education of sexologists on Kinsey, when Kinsey was a dirty old man?"*

Since Americans left the "pre-Kinsey era" behind and plunged headlong into the "post-Kinsey era," what has this meant for all of us? *Stolen Honor, Stolen Innocence, Stolen Family, Stolen America* will, I believe, give you enlightening—and motivating—answers. <u>Today The Kinsey Institute at Indiana University still receives millions of dollars in grants and, through the world's "sex educators," trains millions of young people in utterly fraudulent immoral Kinseyan sexuality</u>. As a citizen, a scholar, a mother, grandmother, and a great- grandmother, it is my fondest hope that the facts you discover here will help you understand the pervasive effects that Prof. Kinsey and Hefner, his personal "pamphleteer," have had on everyone's lives, and inspire you to end their demonic influence on your children and grandchildren. Thank you for caring—and, I pray, rising up and taking action.

AUTHOR'S INTRODUCTION NOTES

1. http://www.infowars.com/glaxosmithkline-fined-over-illegal-vaccine-experiments-killing-14-babies. See also the Guatemala expose as well as those I have written on elsewhere.
2. "Human Rights Campaign Foundation," Buying Guide: http://www.hrc.org/files/assets/resources/2012_BuyersGuide.pdf
3. http://www.huffingtonpost.com/vicki-larson/porn-and-divorce_b_861987.html
4. http://groups.yahoo.com/group/FathersRightsNetwork-International/message/1254
5. http://articles.businessinsider.com/2012-02-21/home/31081751_1_illegitimacy-black-children-unmarried-women# ixzz215ffHhme

Why This Book? why Now?

6 http://futureofchildren.org/publications/journals/article/index.xml?journalid=37&articleid=105&sectionid=674 and http://www.msnbc.msn.com/id/15835429/ns/health-pregnancy/t/nearly-us-babies-born-out-wedlock/#.UAbWGvUnC8U

7 http://www.ewtnnews.com/catholic-news/US.php?id=358

8 http://chastity.com/chastity-qa/stds/infections/how-many-stds-are-there/how-many

9 http://thefatherlessgeneration.wordpress.com/statistics

10 http://www.infowars.com/boy-scouts-were-keeping-policy-banning-gays

11 See Liberty Counsel Researcher Donna Gallagher for documentation of Kinsey Institute funding, www.LC.org.

12 See, Howard Kurtz, "$743,371 Later,'" Washington Post, Sept. 12, 1986.

AMERICA
DARK SLIDE-BRIGHT FUTURE

PART I

KINSEY'S PERSONAL INFLUENCES

CHAPTER 1
KINSEY THE MAN

How was it possible for a sickly, religious boy who grew up to be a serious college student with an obvious talent for biology and an abysmal ignorance of sex—how did this young man evolve into a world authority on sexual behavior who could be mentioned in the same breath with Freud?[1]

Wardell Pomeroy, Kinsey coauthor, 1972

KINSEY BIOGRAPHY

Alfred Charles Kinsey was born in Hoboken, New Jersey, on June 23, 1894. He grew up in South Orange, and was 16 when Congress halted the traffic in young girls ("White Slave Trade") in 1910.

Kinsey was sickly, "frail and not by nature or experience a toughie." Cornelia Christenson continues in *Kinsey: A Biography* that he was not "an able bodied man" and was ineligible to serve in World War I "due to his physical condition, a double curvature of the spine and a possibly defective heart ...caused by rickets in his childhood... bouts of rheumatic fever and even typhoid."[1] He felt "physically inferior to other boys" and was the "shyest guy around girls you could think of."[2] Christenson and others have noted that Kinsey inscribed a line from Shakespeare's *Hamlet* under his high school yearbook photograph: "Man delights me not; no, nor woman either." Pomeroy asks (without answering):

> How was it possible for a sickly, religious boy who grew up to be a serious college student with an obvious talent for biology and an abysmal ignorance of sex—how did this young man evolve into a world authority on sexual behavior who could be mentioned in the same breath with Freud?[3]

Pomeroy, Christenson, and Indiana University (where Kinsey's sex-research operations were based) claim that Kinsey was asexual, disinterested in sex, and celibate prior to marrying in 1921. But in 1997, James H. Jones, another pro-Kinsey biographer who had also received support from the University, revealed startling new details about Kinsey's sexual obsessions in his book, *Alfred C. Kinsey: A Public/Private Life* (hereafter *Alfred C. Kinsey*). Interviewed for a 1998 British television program entitled "Kinsey's Paedophiles," Jones asserted:

> There is no way that the American public in the 1940s and the 1950s would have sanctioned any form of behavior that violated middle class morality on the part of the scientist who was telling the public that he was disinterested and giving them the simple truth... Any disclosure of any feature of this private life that violated middle class morality would have been catastrophic for his career... For Kinsey, life in the closet came complete with a wife, children, a public image... that again he preserved at all costs. Kinsey's reputation still in large measure rests upon an image of him that he cultivated during his lifetime... the official mystique. (Yorkshire Television (Channel 4), United Kingdom, August 10, 1998.)

Another major influence on Kinsey was Charles Darwin, the English naturalist who is credited with formulating the theory of evolution in such works as *The Origin of Species* (1859).[4] Kinsey was so impressed with Darwin's scientific acumen that, upon graduating *magna cum laude* from Bowdoin in 1916, he quoted him in his commencement address.[5]

Following graduation, from Bowdoin College, Kinsey continued his studies at Harvard's Bussey Institution, which was a hotbed of Darwinism and the "New Biology" that led scientists to envision improving the human species through "eugenics." Jones identifies Kinsey as one of the scholarly pre-World War II eugenicists who issued a "terrifying" call for the *mass* sterilization of *"lower level"* Americans and a breeding plan for superior classes.[6]

Sir Thomas Huxley (1825-1895), the foremost proponent of Darwinism in England, was credited by Kinsey with crafting a scientific "declaration of independence."[7] Kinsey claimed to agree with Huxley's dogged determination to accept only those "facts" which could be confirmed via the scientific method. No other authority (including church and state) was accepted.

Kinsey would also play in the same elite eugenic league as Sir Thomas Huxley's grandsons, Aldous and Julian. Sir Julian Huxley, a geneticist and first director-general of UNESCO (United Nations Educational, Scientific, and Cultural Organization) became acquainted with Kinsey's work through Indiana University President Herman Wells. In 1932, Aldous Huxley wrote *Brave New World*, which became required reading in many American schools. It is often misunderstood as "science fiction," but was actually an exposé of the cosmopolitan eugenic vision of state-controlled free love and selective breeding.

As "shy" as he was around women, Kinsey was much at home with young boys. He preferred their company in both outdoor and indoor settings. He joined the Boy Scouts at about age 17, and later as a married man continued to wear his Scout uniform, take boys on nature hikes and the like, and sleep alongside them in tents. Claiming that Kinsey's obsession with boys was entirely platonic,

Pomeroy and Christenson insist that he led a largely sexless life. Evidence from Kinsey's own writings, however, raised serious questions about his sexual orientation long before publication of Jones' *Alfred C. Kinsey* confirmed his deviancy. Even in college he opted for the companionship of youths and boys.

A report by Patrick Boyle, author of *Scout's Honor: Sexual Abuse in America's Most Trusted Institution*, describes Kinsey's role in removing a warning about masturbation from the Scout handbook. According to Boyle, an early edition of the handbook advised Scoutmasters:

Because boys of Scouting age are naturally curious about sex, you may... discover or hear about incidents of sexual experimentation among troop members... Incidents of sexual experimentation call for a private and thorough investigation, and frank discussion with those involved.

Boyle recalls Kinsey's response when the BSA sought his advice for updating the manual in 1947:

Our years of research have failed to disclose any clear cut cases of harm resulting from masturbation, although we have thousands of cases of boys who have had years of their lives ruined by worry over masturbation... We should be glad to serve wherever the Boy Scouts can use factual material," he wrote. The BSA later dropped the discussion of masturbation from its handbook.[8]

This Kinsey-backed move increased the vulnerability of young Scouts to sexual abuse by older peers and adult pederasts, from that time to the present day.

One day when he was about five years of age, Kinsey's son, Bruce, saw a flower and exclaimed, "Look at the pretty flower, Daddy. God made it." Kinsey could not let it pass. "Now Bruce," he said, "where did the flower really come from?" "From a seed," Bruce dutifully replied, apparently aware of the answer that would please his father.[9] There was the implication that if one believes in God, one cannot believe in seeds.

A later incident, while Kinsey was mentoring his sexology disciples, further underscored his atheism. He and Pomeroy were talking about theological matters. Pomeroy, puzzled by the impression "that [Kinsey] still entertained religious feelings," interjected, "I've known you a long time and I've never heard you talk this way. Do you really believe in God?" Kinsey was irate and "surprised" that Pomeroy could have thought for an instant that he was a believer. "Don't be ridiculous. Of course not," he snapped.[10] According to Pomeroy, Kinsey became an atheist shortly after he prayed for divine intervention for the college "friend" (who was Kinsey himself) who could not stop masturbating:

> Kinsey began to lose his beliefs as a college student, when his study of science disclosed to him what he saw as a basic incongruity between it and religion. Having so decided for himself, he could not understand why every other scientist did not think as he did.[11]

Kinsey sought thereafter to avoid those who believed in God. Members of his carefully selected staff were disbelievers. Years later, his *Male* and *Female* volumes would blame religious-based "ancient taboos" for America's supposedly repressive sexual attitudes and resulting social disorders:

> Our particular systems certainly go back to the Old Testament philosophy on which the Talmud is based, and which was the philosophy of those Jews who first followed the Christian faith. In many details, the prescriptions of the Talmud are nearly identical with those of our present-day legal codes governing sexual behavior.[12]

CHAPTER 1 NOTES

1. Cornelia Christenson, *Kinsey: A Biography*, Indiana University, Bloomington, 1971, p. 16.
2. Christenson, p. 19.
3. Dr. Wardell Pomeroy, *Kinsey and The Institute for Sex Research*, Harper & Row, New York, 1972, p. 21.
4. *The Concise Columbia Encyclopedia*, Columbia University Press, 1991.
5. Christenson, p. 30.
6. James H. Jones, *Alfred C. Kinsey: A Public/Private Life*, W. W. Norton, New York, 1997, p. 194, 809 f. 78.
7. Jones, p. 190.
8. Pomeroy, p. 12.
9. Pomeroy, p. 29.
10. Pomeroy, p. 29.
11. Pomeroy, p. 29.
12. Kinsey, Pomeroy, and Martin, *Sexual Behavior in the Human Male*, W.B. Saunders Co., 1948, Philadelphia, p. 465.

CHAPTER 2
THE KINSEY CONNECTIONS

Kinsey's ACLU attorney, Morris Ernst, was a key Planned Parenthood lawyer, while Kinseyan Dr. Mary Calderone had served as medical director of Planned Parenthood. Dr. Calderone was a founder and first *executive director of the Sex (now Sexuality) Information and Education Council of the United States (SIECUS). Mary Calderone and Kinsey co-author, Paul Gebhard, would be very influential authorities in the Roe v. Wade decision.*

Dr. Judith Reisman

KINSEY TIES TO SEXUAL PERVERSION

Neither Kinsey nor members of his team can properly be termed "scientists." Replication and validation are two key attributes of authentic scientific investigation, but Kinsey's data have yet to be validated, and his methodology has not been replicated. One wonders how it could be. Would the abusive treatment of infants and children that became a sordid hallmark of the Kinsey investigation be tolerated today, even in the name of "science"? Subjects of all ages were anonymous, some coerced, and data were clandestinely altered and destroyed at whim.

As with the discredited turn-of-the-century "science" of phrenology, which entailed measuring bumps on the head to estimate intelligence and other traits, the "new academic discipline"[1] of sexology is a shaman's trade; its claim of sound "methodology" is hokum. No sensitive-or sensible-person, including a scientist, who understands the dynamics of marriage, real human love, and the absolute trust and commitment they require, would propose or participate in perverse studies such as those conducted by Alfred Kinsey and his team.

Kinsey claimed his intrusive list of 350 sexual questions had been approved by the Indiana University Board of Trustees.[2] He also insisted that his interview technique elicited "detailed and accurate information from an enormous variety of subjects regarding their most intimate experiences- experiences that many of them had never before "verbalized to another person."[3] But he and his team regularly rejected normal sexual behavior, exhibiting disbelief, contempt, and other negative reactions toward subjects who refused to participate in perverted acts.

Kinsey and his team expressly focused on, and solicited, "units" brought together by common deviant and perverse sexual interests, while feigning to *exclude* groups "brought together by a common sexual interest."[4] They were found in bars, bathhouses, "tearooms,"[5] and "rooming houses." Pomeroy writes,

> [His] first assignment originated with a trip Kinsey made to New York for the purpose of taking the histories of a homosexual group consisting chiefly of writers, artists, architects and others occupied with creative work. This group held frequent sex sessions, to one of which Kinsey was invited as an observer.[6]

Pomeroy then describes the films Kinsey made of numerous homosexual "units" performing sodomy and sexual sadism. As discussed earlier, Kinsey even paid to have two males fly to Bloomington to be filmed performing sadistic sex acts.[7] As described by Pomeroy,

> On subsequent New York trips we spent many hours in gay bars.8 Gebhard was once taking histories in a famous music school where we knew there were a great many homosexuals... [O]ften... we would plunge into a subculture that was unknown to people... the world of homosexual prostitution in the Times Square area of New York... [I]n the evening we took homosexual histories from the Near North Side... His [Kinsey's] mission in Chicago was to collect homosexual histories... [S]oon he had half-dozen centers in the city from which he could make contacts.9

We now have admissions by members of the Kinsey team that Pomeroy was dissembling. Kinsey did not merely "observe" and record homosexual sex on these trips; he was an active, obsessed, and irrational participant.

Kinsey's conjured numbers were the basis for his apocryphal attribution of high rates of sexual perversion among "college level" males, who were viewed as the nation's leadership class. Yet his own writings reveal that *real* college students, rare in his sample, were far more traditional:

> I have been going to the State Penal Farm at Putnamville two or three times every week for the last two months and shall continue so through most of the winter. I have 110 histories from inmates there and can get as many hundreds more as I want... More important... these histories are giving me a look-in on a lower social level, *and the patterns of sexual behavior are totally different from those of college students*. After all, our college students constitute less than 1% of the population and it is the great mass of the population which is reported in the group that I am now working.[10] [Emphasis added.]

To justify his interest in prison and homosexual/city populations, Kinsey claimed on one hand that college students represent only one percent of the population. On the other, he defined the term "college level" so loosely that many of his aberrant populations easily qualified, thereby giving him an excuse to claim that the college level category was the largest sampled. He wrote:

> Again it should be emphasized that most of these calculations of validity have been based on the college segment of the population, which is the only group represented now by large enough series to warrant such examination. [11]

Fortunately, Kinsey's findings were *not* duplicated in the work of Drs. Phyllis and Eberhard Kronhausen, the sexually radical couple[12] who also worked to free the world from sexual repression. Their "erotic" museum in Holland and, in an effort to further Kinsey's cause, conducted a sex survey of 200 male college students which they reported in their book *Sex Histories of American College Men* (1960). But whereas Kinsey sought to create the impression that "college level" men were virtual clones of prison populations, the Kronhausens found that even as late as 1960 Joe College was commonly a virgin:

> NO SEX WITHOUT LOVE: Many of the students were as blushingly romantic about sex morals as any girl of their age would be. To these young men, sex without love seemed utterly unethical. Some of them did not even think it right to kiss a girl unless they were "in love."[13]

> PREMARITAL INTERCOURSE: In the college group as a whole one still finds considerable resistance toward premarital intercourse. What has changed in terms of sex mores between the attitudes of the older generation... [has been]

The Kinsey Connections

as Kinsey puts it, the "rationalizations" which serve to justify this resistance against premarital intercourse.

In our sample: premarital intercourse is considered highly objectionable for reasons which are primarily derived from religious tenets and beliefs and... overvaluation of virginity with particular respect to the female. This overvaluation of female virginity also prevails in the lower educational groups but there it is apparently not taken quite as seriously as in the upper educational groups... [I]t remains a fact that this group engages in relatively little premarital sexual intercourse... *The average modern college man is apt to say that he considers intercourse "too precious" to have with anyone except the girl he expects to marry and may actually abstain from all intercourse for that reason.*

In keeping with this philosophy, the typical college man will say that he feels that marriages work out better if there has been no premarital intercourse and considers himself much "emancipated" as compared to the previous generation because, to him, his reasoning appears to be sounder than that of the older group. However, as Kinsey remarks, this change in the form of their rationalizations has not affected the overt behavior of the two generations in the least.[14] [Emphasis added.]

Even by 1960, the Kronhausens found that oral sodomy was rare among college males, while anal sodomy and bestiality (intercourse with animals) was unheard of. And while Kinsey had claimed "the homosexual incidence at college age to be about 20 percent," the Kronhausens found that only *one-half of one percent* (one in 200 college men) could be considered homosexual.

The Kronhausens caught the fact that Kinsey did not report on "college men," but on "college level" men, "including those younger

13

males who will ultimately go to college, those in college, and those having had college background." Hence, the embarrassing secret of the sexual libertarians was that as much as the Kronhausens wanted to justify Kinsey's claims of widespread sexual promiscuity among college males, they were unable even by 1960 to locate such activity on campus. Not until a decade of *Playboy* (which was launched December 1953), and indoctrination of the pertinent professions (education, psychiatry, psychology, health, law, and the mass communications and entertainment media) with Kinseyan sexuality training, did a dramatically changed societal attitude begin to take place.

Kinsey's revolutionary focus on "orgasm" to measure sexual, marital, dating, and general emotional satisfaction, has become so accepted in the Western world that it is no longer questioned. Yet, while there is a body of literature confirming that orgasm is helpful in marriage, it has never been shown to be a valid measure of sexual success or marital bliss. The data on pedophiles, rapists, and rapist-murderers[15] indicate that while the perpetrators commonly began "petting" to orgasm as youths, their libidos soon required more danger and perversion to attain orgasmic release. The goal may be "orgasm," but the method often becomes increasingly antisocial and violent.

Which "other perversions" beyond homosexuality would Kinsey make respectable, and what was standing in his way? The latter included organized religion, organized American women, and a truly free press. Aided by small newspapers in every city, town, and hamlet, the women of the Purity Movement had brought to a screeching halt the golden profits of the prostitution traffic nationwide. A still virtuous and reading public, which understood its role in self-government, brought legislators to heel. From the Comstock Act of 1873 to the Mann Act of 1910, "physicians and purity crusaders"[16] brought about public awareness and control of venereal disease, prostitution, pedophiles and other forms of vice. With Prohibition (1920-1933),[17] the American people demonstrated their capacity for action as they sought to cripple the traffic in alcohol, and thereby curb the related problems of obscenity, brothels, and drug dealing which posed threats to the institutions of marriage and family, and to the nation.

KINSEY TIES TO CRIMINALS

For his database, Kinsey classified more than 1,400 criminals and sex offenders as "normal,"[18] on grounds that such miscreants are essentially the same as normal men. By doing so, he bolstered the belief that reported increases in sex crimes are spurious; the result of sexually disturbed police or repressive "reform groups." In his *Female* volume, he wrote,

> Preliminary analyses of our data indicate that only a minute fraction of one per cent of the persons who are involved in sexual behavior which is contrary to the law are ever apprehended, prosecuted, or convicted, and that there are many other factors besides the behavior of the apprehended individual which are responsible for the prosecution of the particular persons who are brought to court. The prodding of some reform group, a newspaper-generated hysteria over some local sex crime, a vice drive which is put on by the local authorities to distract attention from defects in their administration of the city government, or the addition to the law-enforcement group of a *sadistic officer who is disturbed over his own sexual problems*, may result in a doubling-a hundred percent increase-in the number of arrests on sex charges, even though there may have been no change in the actual behavior of the community, and even though the illicit sex acts that are apprehended and prosecuted may still represent no more than a fantastically

minute part of the illicit activity which takes place every day in the community.[19] [Emphasis added.]

Kinsey associate Paul Gebhard explained that even the prison sample was heavily weighted toward sexual perversion, since the Kinsey team specifically sought the worst sex offenders:

> At the Indiana State Farm we had no plan of sampling-we simply sought out sex offenders and, after a time, avoided the more common types of offense (e.g. statutory rape) and directed our efforts toward the rarer types. In the early stages of the research, when much interviewing was being done at Indiana correctional institutions, Dr. Kinsey did not view the inmates as a discrete group that should be differentiated from people outside; instead, he looked upon the institutions as reservoirs of potential interviewees, **literally captive subjects**. *This viewpoint resulted in there being no differentiation in our 1948 volume between persons with and without prison experience. . . .* the great majority of the prison group was collected omnivorously without any sampling plan-we simply interviewed all who volunteered and when this supply of subjects was exhausted we solicited other inmates essentially at random... Kinsey... never... [kept] a record of refusal rates-the proportion of those who were asked for an interview but who refused.[20] [Emphasis added.].

Kinsey claimed that convicted criminals, including sex offenders, were no different than most men, they had merely been caught. Included in his "human males" sample were incarcerated pedophiles, pederasts (homosexual pedophiles), homosexual males, boy prostitutes, and other social and sexual outlaws. Yet the team regularly wrote and testified to the "average" nature of their male sample – just like dad. Kinsey coauthor Paul Gebhard admitted as much:

> Kinsey did mix male prison inmates in with his sample used in *Sexual Behavior in Human Male... As* to generalizing to a wider population, in his first volume Kinsey did generalize to the entire U.S. population. See, for one example, the tables on page 188 and 220 where he clearly extrapolates to the U.S. Subsequently he realized this error and no such extrapolation is found in his second volume.[21]

Another 300 aberrant subjects were selected from a population Kinsey called "the underworld," which he defined as persons "*[d]eriving a significant portion of their income from illicit activities: e.g., bootleggers, con men, dope peddlers, gamblers, hold-up men, pimps, prostitutes, etc.*"[22] For Kinsey, the only sex crimes which qualified as "underworld" were those that involved economic gain, such as prostitution and pandering.

KINSEY TIES TO DARWIN

When Magnus Hirschfeld addressed the First International Conference for Sexual Reform held in Berlin in 1921, he reminded his audience that the term "sexual science" derived from Charles Darwin's *The Descent of Man* and Ernst Haeckel's *Natuerliche Schofungsgeschicte*. (E. Michael Jones, *Culture Wars*, "Magnus Hirschfeld and the Gay Science," September 1997, Vol. 16, #9, pages 30-43.)

The Kinsey team understood and portrayed human sexual behavior as a closed Darwinian system of simple mammalian behavior: a stimulus provided, followed by a genital response, produces an orgasmic "outlet." Kinsey applied Pavlovian conditioning to sex, contending that *all* sex is conditioned by environment, and that love, jealously, fear, anger, shame, and similar emotions have no operational meaning independent of sex. From the start, Kinsey denied explanations for human behavior that conflicted with his evolutionary assumptions. He enthusiastically utilized research techniques appropriate for the study of insects for his evaluation of human sexual behavior.[23]

> The techniques of this research [have been] born out of the senior author's longtime experience with a problem in insect taxonomy. The transfer from insect to human material is not illogical, for it has been a transfer of a method that may be applied to the study of any variable population, in any field. The sex studies were on a very different scale from the insect studies where we had 150,000 individuals available for the study of a single species of gall wasp.[24]

In a review of Reisman's earlier book, *Kinsey, Sex and Fraud* (Reisman, *et al*), the respected British medical journal *The Lancet* summarized Kinsey's *qualitative* and q*uantitative* research findings as follows: (1)"any questionnaire survey in a normally private area is subject to bias from differences in those who respond and those who refuse, and there is no ready means of checking the information"; and (2) Kinsey *et al* "questioned an unrepresentative proportion of prison inmates and sex offenders in a survey of 'normal' sexual behavior." In its March 1991 issue, *The Lancet* also noted that Kinsey's "methodology" involved "unethical, possibly criminal, observations of children."[25]

KINSEY TIES TO GERMAN NAZIS

The Kinsey Institute and the University contend to this day that Kinsey began gathering sexuality data after 1938 so that he could accurately answer questions posed by students about marriage and family life. Yet he was well aware of the wealth of available information on the subject. He was, for instance, familiar with the work of Dr. Magnus Hirschfeld. Kinsey's friend (and father of the transgender movement), Dr. Harry Benjamin,[26] had brought Hirschfeld to America to speak against the social reform accomplishments of the Purity Movement.[27] In 1919, Hirschfeld established the world's first Institute for Sexology in Berlin, organizing it into four departments: Sexual Biology, Sexual Medicine, Sexual Sociology, and Sexual Ethnology.[28] Englishman Christopher Isherwood wrote about life in Berlin at the time, from which the stage production and movie *Caberet* was drawn. Isherwood, a pederast, summarized his view of Germany as "Berlin is for boys."[29]

In his autobiography, *Christopher and His Kind, 1929-1939*, Isherwood describes the activities and events at Hirschfeld's Institute, including the incongruity of respectable elegance in the dining hall while another chamber featured "live exhibits... whips, chains and other sexual torture instruments" routinely used in "therapy" by Hirschfeld's "patients," Nazis, and others. Isherwood notes that Hirschfeld publicly advocated sex between consenting individuals, including adult sex with older children.[30] He urged "tolerance" and called Americans sexual "hypocrites"-terms later popularized by Kinsey in a similar U.S. context.

Hirschfeld complained that U.S. attitudes toward sex were not "scientific." Dr. Benjamin hoped to have Hirschfeld lead an American sexual reform movement, but apparently the publicly- acknowledged homosexual German sexologist did not fit the profile that U.S. society would trust. Midwestern "family man" Kinsey would eventually fill the void.

Yorkshire investigators had followed up Dr. Reisman's original questions regarding Kinsey's association with Nazis and the possibility that some of the abused children were obtained from WWII Germany and/or Russia. At least one of Kinsey's sex collaborators was a documented Nazi, the infamous George Sylvester Viereck, a convicted German spy who had worked among Washington D.C. power brokers. David Brinkley in his history of the period, *Washington Goes to War* (1988:26) wrote that Viereck was "one of the...masterminds of the propaganda cabinet that Germany set up here early in the war." Yorkshire researchers flew to Berlin (as did this author), interviewing and digging through old files and press reports. There they discovered Dr. Friedrich Karl Hugo Viktor von Balluseck, who was tried in Berlin in 1957 for a child sex murder. According to Paul Gebhard who took over serving as the prestigious Director of Indiana University's Kinsey Institute, just after Kinsey's death:

> [Kinsey] wrote him questions in the letter and they carried on quite a correspondence... Police [seeking a child sex murderer] went through his possessions... found his correspondence with Kinsey... They got Interpol... The FBI put pressure on Kinsey to reveal the guy's sexual diary. Kinsey said, absolutely not. [T]he poor paedophile... had his reputation destroyed... finally quit corresponding with us.

Like Kinsey, fascist scientists in Germany[31] believed that they had a right to experiment on anyone. Dr. von Balluseck[32] was an incest offender who raped and sodomized not only his own offspring, but Jewish, Polish, and German children as well, from roughly 1927 to 1957. The German press reported Kinsey's visit to Frankfort during his world tour in 1956. Little else is available regarding the German stopover, or if Kinsey met with Balluseck, and there was no mention of Kinsey's visit to Frankfort in the approved writings about Kinsey's European travels.

Dr. von Balluseck's trial for the murder of 10-year-old Loiselotte Has, who was "found... naked and throttled... on a piece of wasteland," was widely covered in Germany. It was "completely unprecedented in the moral history of the post war era," and von Balluseck was described as "the most important pedophile in the criminal history of Berlin." Kinsey collaborator Balluseck was tried for the abuse of 50, or "more than 100," or "several hundred" children.

As noted, he had sexually violated children for "over the last three decades" (*Frankfurter Allgemeine Zeitung*, May 22, 1957).

News of Kinsey's role in the case was splashed across the headlines of Germany's largest newspapers. Judge Heinrich Berger "emphasized again and again the important function played by the press in warning the public against paedophiles like Balluseck, who approach children as understanding friends and helpers in their sexual need" (*Frankfurter Allgemeine Zeitung*, May 22, 1957). Despite Alfred Kinsey's shocking role in the explosive case, the U.S. press was uniformly silent about it.

According to Yorkshire Television's research department, from 1942 to 1944 Dr. von Balluseck was the Department of Justice District Kreishauptmina, the commandant of the small Polish town of Jedrzejow. It was there that he targeted the children he sexually assaulted, warning them, according to German news accounts, that "It is either the gas chamber or me." *The Encyclopedia Judaica* [33] reports that all Jedrejow Jews ended up in the gas chambers. All, including the children, were under the control of Herr von Balluseck.

The German press described early attempts to "cover up" who Balluseck really was, including efforts to keep his photograph under wraps and the court description of the influential attorney as a "shop-worker." And commenting on the experiments recorded in volumes found in von Balluseck's desk, Judge Berger exclaimed: "This is no longer human! What was this all for? To tell Kinsey about?" (*Morgenpost*, May 16, 1957). Here are additional excerpts from German press accounts:

> The Nazis knew and gave him the opportunity to practice his abnormal tendencies in occupied Poland on Polish children, who had to choose between Balluseck and the gas

ovens. After the war, the children were dead, but Balluseck lived. [*National-Zeitung,* May 15, 1957]

Balluseck's career catapulted because he was a fanatical member of the Nazi party... he was a Nazi Occupational officer in Poland and he abused 10-12 year old girls. [*Neues Deustschland,* May 17, 1957]

Balluseck... corresponded with the American Kinsey Institute for some time, and had also got books from them which dealt with child sexuality [*Tagespiegel,* October 1, 1957]

[N]ot only did he commit his crimes in Germany, but also during the war as an occupation officer, he committed numerous sexual crimes against Polish girls of between 10 & 14 years old. [*Der Morgen,* May 15, 1957]

Dr. Balluseck... [recorded measurements] of his crimes committed against children between 9 and 14 years old... in four thick diaries... of a pseudo-scientific character... while in correspondence with the American sexual researcher Kinsey... about his research results which as he said himself, took place over three decades. [*Frankfurter Allgemeine Zeitung,* May 22, 1957]

Judge Berger: "I had the impression that you got to the children in order to impress Kinsey and to deliver him material."

Balluseck: "Kinsey himself asked me for that [asked me to do so]"

As a role model for his perverse actions Balluseck named the so-called sexual psychologist Kinsey... [*Neuess Deutschland,* May, 17, 1957]

Today the court has got four diaries, and in these diaries, with cynicism and passion, he recorded his crimes against 100 children in the smallest detail. He sent the detail of his experiences regularly to the US sex researcher, Kinsey. The latter was very interested and kept up a regular and lively correspondence with Balluseck [*National-Zeitung*, May 15, 1957]

Sharp criticism of American sex researcher by presiding Judge... Heinrich Berger... because of the correspondence between Regierungsrat Dr. Fritz von Balluseck, accused of many counts of sexual crimes, and Kinsey. The presiding judge exclaimed, *"Instead of answering his sordid letters, the strange American scholar should rather have made sure that Mister von Balluseck was put behind bars."* [*Morgenpost*, May 16, 1957]

The connection with Kinsey, towards whom he'd showed off his crimes, had a disastrous effect on [von Balluseck]... [I]n his diaries he'd stuck in the letters from the sex researcher, Kinsey in which he'd been *encouraged to continue* his research... He had also started relationships... *to expand his researches.* One shivers to think of the lengths he went to. [*TSP*, May 17, 1957, emphasis added]

Indeed, the German press reported that Post WW II von Balluseck sexually assaulted his own daughter, and the 11-year-old son of a vicar, and forced the boy to write down the acts for Kinsey.

Kinsey had asked the paedophile specifically for material of his perverse actions. The presiding judge, Dr. Berger noted that it was Kinsey's duty to get Balluseck locked up, instead of corresponding with him. [*Berliner Zeitung*, May 16, 1957]

He made statistics of all these experiences and he sent them with comprehensive reports to the American sex researcher, Kinsey. In one reply, which apart from a "thank you," contained the warning "be careful" (or "watch out") Balluseck cut out the signature from this letter, and stuck it in his diary. [*TGSP,* May 16, 19957]

In the diaries, described as volume 1 & 4, he described with pedantic exactness, how he com- mitted his crimes... Balluseck had close contact with the so called American sex researcher, Kinsey, to whom he'd repeatedly and explicitly reported his perverse crimes. Balluseck had also described those in pedantic detail in his diaries. [*National-Zeitung,* May 15, 1957]

So Balluseck was not only sending Kinsey his old child abuse data, recorded during his days as a Commandant in Jedrzejow; he was also seeking to "continue" and "expand" his sexual seduction of children for Kinsey's use.

The University of Indiana press office regularly forwards international articles about the school (especially those containing damaging information) to the administration. According to Paul Gebhard, the University and its president, Herman Wells, were aware of Kinsey's collaboration with Balluseck. Kinsey refused to provide evidence that the FBI knew he had regarding Balluseck's crimes.

After serving his sentence for massive child sex abuse (he was not convicted on the murder charge), Balluseck continued his correspondence with Gebhard, while the latter indignantly protested that this "poor pedophile" had trouble obtaining a job after his release from prison.

During a seminar on *The Ethics of Sex Research* (Masters, Johnson & Kolodny, 1972), Gebhard told the assembled sexology "experts" that it was ethical to use Balluseck's child data. None registered disagreement, nor did any protest when Gebhard revealed how the Kinsey team had covered up for the erstwhile Nazi.

> We [were] amoral at best and criminal at worst... An example of our criminality is our refusal to cooperate with authorities in apprehending a pedophile we had interviewed who was being sought for a [child] sex murder.[34]

The sort of conjecture that enabled the Yorkshire researchers to uncover Balluseck's connection to Kinsey seems once again in order. Were some of Kinsey's 317 to 2,035 boys and girls mentioned in the *Male* and *Female* volumes exterminated in Treblinka? Were sexually abused and murdered children included in the records that Balluseck "repeatedly and explicitly" mailed to Kinsey? If so, and it is highly likely, these war-crime "data" have been used by psychopathic sexual revolutionaries to uproot American laws and culture.

By 1933, the German euthanasia program was under way and the groundwork was laid for un- conscionable human experiments on adults and children. Dachau had been established with over 8,000 slaves, who were routinely rented out by the Nazi government to private farms, factories, and institutions. Some would likely have gone to research laboratories at the Kaiser Wilhelm Institute:

> From 1933 to 1945 the expenses for the SS for one inmate averaged about ten cents a day. That included board, clothing, "supervision," housing. Inmates were rented out to private industry at the price of $1 a day or, for skilled workers, $1.50 a day. That made a huge profit for the SS, which, as is often overlooked, became a very big commercial undertaking itself and also piled up enormous profits for the private industrial corporations from the cheap labor...

Inmates had to work long hours—usually eleven hours—including Sundays and holidays.[35]

Nazi Germany was a "police state," and Pomeroy tells us that Kinsey "would have done business with the devil himself if it would have furthered the research."[36] George Sylvester Viereck, the convicted World War II traitor and Kinsey correspondent, was the "devil" to whom Pomeroy was referring. Viereck worked for the German embassy in Washington, D.C. David Brinkley, in *Washington Goes to War* (1988), recalls that he was on Hitler's payroll as a conduit of information to and from "Hitler using money from Germany to set up... Nazi front groups."[37]

KINSEY TIES TO PLANNED PARENTHOOD

Virtually without exception, the basis of professional sexual training is Kinsey's duplicitous data, and that of his disciples who have built upon the false foundation he established.

From the "informal" sex education reaching nearly all children via pornography, to the "formal" sex education from doctorate to kindergarten, the Kinsey Model is the monopoly. The foundation of the modern sex industry then, from sex commerce to the sex "expert" who serve as expert witnesses for pornographers, all stand on the legitimacy of wholly illegitimate, criminal pseudoscience. Next we will examine how this "education" process has been used to reshape our laws on sex offenses, to fit the Kinsey Model, impacting the lives of every American.

One of several other "special interest" associations whose economic and social base now includes "sexuality instruction" is the *American Association of Marriage and Family Counselors*. The current decisions by the *American Psychiatric Association* (1994) in its *Diagnostic and Statistical Manual IV* to remove pedophilia, masochism and sadism as mental or psychological disorders and a 1999 article in the *American Psychological Association Bulletin* which would normalize adult sex with "willing" children, means these two powerful mental health agencies have joined forces with Kinsey's other pedophile advocates.[38]

Kinsey's ACLU attorney, Morris Ernst, was a key Planned Parenthood lawyer, while, as noted, Kinseyan Dr. Mary Calderone had served as medical director of Planned Parenthood. Dr. Calderone was a founder and first executive director of SIECUS. She and Kinsey co-author, Paul Gebhard, would be very influential authorities in the *Roe v. Wade* decision. Roe includes a footnote citation to Draft No. 9 (May 8, 1959) of the American Law Institute-Model Penal Code (ALI-MPC), which in turn states: "Major sources of Information on abortion include two sources: Calderone, *Abortion in the United States* (1958); Gebhard and others, *Pregnancy, Birth and Abortion*, chap. 8 (1958)."[39]

In their book, *Blessed are the Barren*, authors Marshall and Donovan reference the famous Kinsey's Planned Parenthood speech,

> At the 1955 abortion conference sponsored by the Planned Parenthood Federation of America... the question of physician-induced abortion came up. The discussion leader on this point was the famed sex researcher, Alfred Kinsey.[40]

In 1965, the late Dr. Abraham Stone and the late Dr. Norman Himes wrote *Planned Parenthood: A Practical Handbook of Birth-Control Methods*. The authors cite:

> The problem of induced abortion in the United States was covered in depth at the 1955 Arden House Conference on Abortion sponsored by the Planned Parenthood Federation of America. *An attempt was made to determine the extent and size of the problem.* The late

> Dr. Alfred C. Kinsey reported to this conference the results obtained by *his group sampling methods*. Abortion data was gathered by the Kinsey group as part of the total record of female sexual activity; the sample reported consisted of 4,248 pregnancies occurring in 5,299 white females. The proportion of *premarital conceptions in this group terminated by induced abortion was in the range of 88 to 95 per cent! Of the married women in the sample, 22 per cent had at least one abortion of an unwanted pregnancy by age forty-five*. Among all the single women who had had coitus, the abortion incidence was 20 per cent.[41]

The attempt to show massive abortions—and the harmlessness of abortions if performed by physicians—required that the Kinsey team find, as they did, that abortions were largely beneficial. They actually improved marriages, and were found safe and morally acceptable to the medical profession. But, to do so meant that almost all abortions had to be carried out by "physicians" with largely favorable results. To accomplish this flight of fancy, the Kinsey team returned to their successful ploy of redefining the common English language—like that of "married" women—which inevitably misled and confused legislators, the public and other scholars, as well as judges and juries.

KINSEY TIES TO EUGENICS AND LEADING EUGENICISTS

Kinsey worked to undermine marriage as a sacrament in which a man and woman commit to each other to generate and nurture new life. This was in keeping with the eugenic thinkers of his day, who sought to remove the "archaic" impediment of the traditional family from the road to their sexual utopia. Kinsey was uniquely qualified for the job of devaluing "pure" women, thereby hamstringing the family. The extensive propagation of his devious data has contributed significantly to the breakdown of heterosexual love, tenderness and parenting. Kinsey's legacy is truly appalling. For the model of the 60s recreational man and woman led directly to the current disorder, despair, disease, and sex crime and deviance among American children.

Both Hermann Muller and Kinsey appeared in the pages of *Sexology*, a pseudo-medical sex journal on whose board sat Kinsey colleagues Harry Benjamin and Rene Guyon. Muller and Kinsey agreed on the need to replace religion with scientific belief and sexual restraint with sexual license. They also shared an enthusiasm for "positive eugenics," the elimination of defective genetic stock by mass sterilization. In *The Human Agenda* (1972), medical ethicist Roderick Gorney connects eugenicist Muller with Aldous Huxley's predictions in *Brave New World:*

> The more radical method of genetic intervention is called "positive eugenics." This is a more ambitious and controversial proposal, championed, among others, by the late Hermann Muller, who [advocates] selective breeding... to eliminate the defects... [and] to increase the number of people with "superior" qualities. One way to accomplish this would be to establish sperm (and eventually egg) banks in which the reproductive cells of individuals with the exceptional health, intelligence, or special talent could be preserved. These could then be used by people who want to produce children with better endowment than would result from their own genes. Some have objected that people would not willingly agree to substitute the sex cells and characteristics of others for their own. Muller rejects "the stultifying assumption that people would have to be forced, rather than inspired, to engage in any effective kind of genetic betterment." He points out that... seemingly "normal couples" ...would elect to use this means of having

at least a part of their family... [T]he obvious successes achieved by this method would within a generation win it still more adherents. It would constitute a major extension of human freedom in a quite new direction.

[Gorney continues] But naturally, such a program poses a potential threat to our values... It opens the door to the frightening abuses of compulsion outlined in Aldous Huxley's *Brave New World*, such as the creation of special classes best fitted to be servants to others who are rulers. With good reason, we might fear the consequences of such a system conducted according to the mad assumptions of racists.[42]

The eugenic power vortex is more fully documented in the book, *Psychiatrists: The Men Behind Hitler*. Authors Roder, Kubillus and Burwell report on a 1962 London symposium on genetics attended by Muller, his fellow Communist comrade and Kinsey's London host, J.B.S. Holdane, Sir Julian Huxley, and others. These "superior" men, like Kinsey, saw themselves as eugenic royalty, or the new genetic hegemony. Their network of interlocking scholarly elitists is one of a mutually supportive cadre for whom the world is their laboratory, thus all "science" is "good" by definition. Under the banner of Darwinian progress, their plans are chilling indeed and they are underway at this moment, good reader, with official sanction, encouragement, and public funds.

Illegally barred from access to the Kinsey archive, "unfriendly" scholars can find no answers about Kinsey's support of Rex King who systematically assaulted over 800 children for Kinsey's *Male* volume. It is absurd to ignore evidence implicating the Rockefeller-German-Russian eugenic network in providing Kinsey's "aides" access to children destined for death in places like *Bushmanshoff*. (Refer to Leverage By Big Money)

Kinsey's personal motive for his research was no mystery. A sexual outlaw himself, he hated the way America's Christian-based law constrained America's sexual and moral life. All nations are inherently religious, even under the mask of atheism. The "Grand Scheme" shared by Kinsey and like-minded eugenic and legal elites, would do no less than gut the Old and New Testaments as America's founding common law order. Kinsey's closeted cadre were at war. They would deconstruct the Common Law, anointing science as the nation's religion and scientists as the new priest class. But, the renowned Jewish authority Rabbi Daniel Lapin, author of *America's Real War* has summarized what is at risk when the Christian roots of this nation are destroyed:

> I desperately want my children, and one day (God willing) my grandchildren and their descendants, to have the option of living peacefully and productively in the United States of America. I am certain this depends upon America regaining its Christian-oriented moral compass... American Jews in particular, owe a debt of gratitude to Christians for the safe haven America has been since its founding.

Kinsey was, no doubt, proud of his key position in the science clergy. In the end, it is not surprising that an official finding of J. Carroll Reece's Congressional Committee's investigation was that the Foundation-sponsored Kinsey Reports were "deliberately designed as an attack on Judaic-Christian morality." Kinsey's human experiments on children give us the glimpse into the widespread, far-reaching network of New Biology scientists while their current traffic in fetal parts hints at where the new/old religion is going. American can no longer deny the reality of what the sexual revolution has wrought here and throughout the world.

America: Dark Slide-Bright Future

CHAPTER 2 NOTES

1. Ethan Bronner, "Study of Sex Experiencing 2nd Revolution," *The New York Times*, December 28, 1997, p. 1.
2. James H. Jones, *The Origins of the Institute for Sex Research*, UMI Dissertation Services, Ann Arbor, Michigan, 1973, pp. 96-99.
3. Pomeroy, Flax and Wheeler, *Taking a Sex History*, The Free Press, New York, 1982, p. 1.
4. Louis Terman, "Kinsey's Sexual Behavior in the Human Male: Some Comments and Criticisms," *Psychological Bulletin 45*, 1948, p. 457.
5. Kinsey, Pomeroy, Martin and Gebhard, *Sexual Behavior in the Human Male*, W.B. Saunders Co., Philadelphia, 1948, p. 93.
6. Laud Humphreys, *Tearoom Trade*, Aldine Publishing Company, New York, 1970, 1975. "Tearooms" are public toilets where homosexual males perform sex acts, often via "glory holes" drilled in the wall of the stalls to allow anonymous sodomy.
7. Wardell Pomeroy, *Dr. Kinsey and the Institute for Sex Research*, Harper & Row, New York, 1972, p. 175.
8. Pomeroy, p. 176.
9. Pomeroy, p. 134.
10. *The Indianapolis Star*, "Kinsey Report May Be Flawed," September 19, 1995, A1, 4., Bancroft said "likely all based on sessions with lone elderly scientist."
11. Cornelia Christenson, *Kinsey: A Biography*, Indiana University, Bloomington, IN., 1971, p. 116.
12. *Male*, p. 153.
13. Eberhard emigrated to the University of Minnesota from Berlin, Germany in 1945.
14. Drs. Phyllis and Eberhard Kronhausen, *Sex Histories of American College Men*, Ballantine Books, New York, 1960, p. 219.
15. See data from The Missing and Exploited Children's Center in Arlington, Virginia and also, Reisman, *Images of Children, Crime and Violence in Playboy, Penthouse and Hustler*, 1989 and *"Soft Porn" Plays Hardball*, 1991. For much of the data on increased violence included in this chapter see William J. Bennett, *The Index of Leading Cultural Indicators*, Empower America, the Heritage Foundation, Free Congress Foundation,

Washington, D.C., Vol. 1, March 1993, pp. 2-22 and Patrick Fagan, *The Root Causes of Violent Crime: The Breakdown of Marriage, Family and Community*, The Heritage Foundation, Washington, DC, B-10265, March 17, 1995.

16. Jones, Kinsey: *A Private/Public Life*, p. 330.
17. Prohibition, 1917-1933.
18. James H. Jones, *Kinsey, A Private/Public Life*, W. W. Norton, New York, 1997, p. 835, f. 40. Urolaglia refers to sexual addiction/arousal from observing people urinate. See also Jack Douglas, *The Family in America*, Mount Morris, IL, The Rockford Institute, May, 1947, pp. 2-4.
19. Wardell Pomeroy, *Dr. Kinsey and the Institute for Sex Research*, Harper & Row, New York, 1972, p. 67.
20. Pomeroy, pp. 68-70.
21. Letter from Paul Gebhard to Director June M. Reinisch at the Kinsey Institute, December 6, 1990. In the author's archive.
22. Kinsey, Pomeroy, Martin and Gebhard, *Sexual Behavior in the Human Male*, W.B. Saunders Co., Philadelphia, 1948, p. 176.
23. Kinsey, Pomeroy and Martin, *Sexual Behavior in the Human Male*, W.B. Saunders, Philadelphia, 1948. Among other citations, Kinsey says here that he used the same techniques for the study of wasps as he did for humans. "The techniques of this research [were] born out of the senior author's longtime experience with [i]nsect[s]. The transfer from insect to human material is not illogical and can be applied to all population studies." (p. 9). This statement is repeated by Hermann Muller about fruit flies. Muller, also a Rockefeller grantee, joined Kinsey's zoology department at IU in 1946.
24. *Male*, 1948, p. 9.
25. *The Lancet*, "Really, Dr. Kinsey?" March 2, 1991, p. 547.
26. James H. Jones, *Alfred C. Kinsey, A Public/Private Life*, W. W. Norton & Company, New York, 1997, p. 741 and Christenson pp. 154, 156 and 215.
27. *San Francisco Examiner*, February 25, 1931, p. 1.
28. Erwin Haeberle, *The Birth of Sexology: A Brief History in Documents, Science and Research*, Berlin, 1983, p. 29. The citation for this publication states: "Research for this project has been supported by The Kinsey Institute for Research in Sex, Gender and Reproduc- tion, Indiana University, Bloomington, Indiana."

30. Christopher Isherwood, *Christopher and His Kind: 1929-1939*, Farrar, Straus, & Giroux, New York, 1976. Isherwood, pp. 17-19.

31. Max Weinreich, *Hitler's Professors: The Part of Scholarship in Germany's Crimes Against the Jewish People*, Yiddish Scientific Institute, Yivo, New York, 1946

32. A photocopy of Dr. von Balluseck's Nazi membership card, dated August 1, 1930, obtained from the German document center, is on file in the author's archive. Max Weinreich, *Hitler's Professors: The Part of Scholarship in Germany's Crimes Against the Jewish People*, Yiddish Scientific Institute--Yivo, New York, 1946

33. *The Encyclopedia Judaica*, Keter Publishing, Vol. 9, 1972, p. 1310-1311.

34. Masters, Johnson, and Kolodny, Ed., *Ethical Issues in Sex Therapy and Research*, Little Brown and Company, Boston, 1977, p. 13.

35. Fredic Wertham, "The German Euthanasia Program," excerpted from *A Sign for Cain*, Hayes Publishing, Cincinnati, Ohio 1973, pp. 14, 15.

36. Kinsey, Pomeroy and Martin, *Sexual Behavior in the Human Male*, W.B. Saunders, Philadelphia, 1948, p. 198.

37. David Brinkley, *Washington Goes to War*, Ballantine Books, New York, 1988, p. 26.

38. Carol Travis, *Uproar Over Sexual Abuse Study Muddies the Waters*, Los Angeles Times, July 19, 1999.

39. Paul Gebhard, Wardell Pomeroy, Clyde Martin and Cornelia Christenson, "Pregnancy, Birth and Abortion," in *Sex Research Studies from the Kinsey Institute*, Martin S. Weinberg, editor, Oxford University Press, New York, 1976, pp. 205-206.

40. Robert Marshall and Charles Donovan, *Blessed are the Barren: The Social Policy of Planned Parenthood*, Ignatius Press, San Francisco, CA, 1991, p. 260.

41. Stone and Himes, Planned Parenthood: A Practical Handbook of Birth Control Methods, Collier Books, New York, 1965, p. 235.

42. Roderick Gorney, *The Human Agenda*, Simon & Schuster, New York, 1972, p. 215.

AMERICA
DARK SLIDE-BRIGHT FUTURE

PART II

POWERFUL LEVERAGE OF KINSEY'S LEGACY

CHAPTER 3
CULTURAL POWER

...by 1950, under cover of the American Bar Association and funded by Carnegie and Rockefeller grants, the tiny cadre of American Law Institute-Model Penal Code authors did not "clarify" America's common law, but rather radically changed its sex laws based on Kinsey's "data."

Dr. Judith Reisman

LEVERAGE BY BIG MONEY

The original patron of the Kinsey research in 1938 was publicly-funded Indiana University. Thereafter, the tax-exempt Rockefeller Foundation backed Kinsey's work through the National Research Council. By the 1960s, the pornography industry, primarily *Playboy*, supported the Kinsey team's "New Biology."

According to the *International Encyclopedia of the Social Sciences* (1968), Kinsey "began his sex research, unassisted, in 1938... Support first came from the National Research Council and the Medical Division of The Rockefeller Foundation."[1] Writing in *Twenty-Five Years of Sex Research, History of the National Research Council Committee for Research in Problems of Sex, 1922-1947*, Sophie D. Aberle and George W. Corner report that the Foundation helped organize and fund the American Social Hygiene Association in 1913 "for reconsideration of public attitudes toward prostitution," and to work for birth control and other social reforms. European and English sex studies were fashionable, and a number of major treatises had been published by men (and a few by women) between 1885 and 1912.

The immense blitz and publicity aroused overwhelming public interest in Kinsey's first book, *Sexual Behavior in the Human Male*, supposedly came as a surprise to its authors and publisher. That is doubtful, however, considering the enormous advance effort to promote it, including efforts of the Rockefeller-connected mass media to effusively hype the book and its culturally corrosive message.

But how did this bow-tied, Midwestern biology professor become a savvy public relations wizard capable of conducting a book promotion rivaling that of a Madison Avenue ad agency? An indication of the answer is found in the record of the Rockefeller Foundation's extensive influence on mass communication. The Rockefeller Foundation funded communications experts from the field of social science to shape pre- and postwar public attitudes.

In 1954, the American Statistical Association (ASA) published *Statistical Problems of the Kinsey Report: A Report of the American Statistical Association Committee to Advise the National Research Council Committee for Research in Problems of Sex*, by Cochran, Mosteller, Tukey and Jenkins. Jones documents the fact that the ASA yielded to unrelenting pressure from the Rockefeller Foundation and the National Research Council to alter their original conclusion that Kinsey's statistics were meaningless.[2]

The Kinsey Institute began collecting obscenity prior to publication of the 1948 *Male* volume. Kinsey received Rockefeller monies for his "library" activities in 1946. Moreover, in his May 7, 1951 letter to "CIB," Warren Weaver complains that Kinsey's "library of erotic literature, and a collection of pictures and other 'art' objects of erotic significance" were essentially funded by Rockefeller.

By 1989, a Rockefeller-funded National Research Council AIDS report said America could be divided into "pre-Kinsey" and "post-Kinsey" eras.[3] The Founders had woven fixed laws and principles into the fabric of the new nation. Kinsey and his associates considered the legal prohibitions and societal restrictions in Judaism and Christianity as "repressive," archaic and harmful. He and his legal colleagues embarked on a voyage to reopen as "new," the old pagan world.

Like Congressman Reece, Supreme Court Justice Louis Brandeis—while supportive of the concept of evolutionary law—was concerned about philanthropies such as the Rockefeller Foundation. He issued this warning about their powerful special-interest influence under the guise of benevolence: *"There develops within the State a state so powerful that the ordinary social and industrial forces existing are insufficient to cope with it... [Their power is] inconsistent with our democratic aspirations."*[4] [Emphasis added.]

The Foundation enthusiastically supported the concept of "eugenics," which encourages the reproductive efforts of those deemed to have "good" ("eu" from the Greek for good) genes, while discouraging or stopping procreation by undesirables. This view had motivated the Foundation's earlier support of Planned Parenthood founder Margaret Sanger, and her eugenic and birth control movement. But Rockefeller and others were anxious to go even further to mold America's breeding patterns along evolutionary lines.

The Rockefeller Foundation considered Kinsey's "quantitative content" sex research of critical importance to the "grand scheme." As Professor Christopher Simpson wrote in *Science of Coercion*: The Foundation sought "quantitative" data to provide "a tool for social management" that is postwar "psychological warfare" with which to impose the will of the elite "on the masses."[5]

While many legislators and judges were concerned about the influence of tax-exempt foundations on American life, The Rockefeller Foundation funded Kinsey and then funded the American Law Institute's production of the Model Penal Code (MPC). The Rockefeller Foundation knew that Kinsey's data, compiled by rapists, incest offenders, pedophiles, homosexuals, prostitutes, etc., were unreliable and criminal. Yet the American Law Institute MPC authors—Wechsler, Ploscowe, Guttmacher, Tappan, and Schwartz—used Kinsey's aberrant criminal population to frame the 1955 model code on sex offenses. The MPC was designed to be sent to state legislatures and especially to influence judges.

By 1955, Kinsey was at the height of his renown. Homosexual author Gore Vidal described him as the "most famous man in America, the world, for about a decade."[6] In the wake of Reece's Congressional Investigation, Dean Rusk, then president of the Rockefeller Foundation (and later Secretary of State) terminated the Foundation's financial support of Kinsey's sex research.[7] Kinsey had served his purpose. The Foundation had shifted its funds to the American Law Institute. There, Kinsey's research would be put to use to erode existing laws protecting women, children, marriage and the family and to craft more lenient sex-offender laws via the American Law Institute's (ALI) Model Penal Code. On April 25, 1955, the ALI released its first Model Penal Code draft (#4), modeled in large part on Kinsey's recommendations, which helped to alter and liberally revise American sex offender laws and penalties.

LEVERAGE IN AMERICAN LAW

Kinsey's Sexual Revolution was not designed just as a trend meant to liberate America's libido by influencing culture, as many may mistakenly think. Rather, Kinsey meant to undermine the legal protections for the institution of marriage, the smallest building block of American society.

Cultural Power

It begins with the influence of these data upon Kinsey's collaborators in the American Law Institute (ALI), founded in 1923. By 1947 the American Bar Association (ABA) joined with the ALI to begin a "national program of continuing education of the bar."⁴ The Model Penal Code produced by the ALI and adopted by the ABA in 1955 was vital to altering our nation's sex-crime statutes, state by state. How influential were Kinsey's data in the preparation of the new penal code?

According to Kinsey's authorized biographer, Jonathan Gathorne-Hardy, "The American Law Institute's *Model Penal Code* of 1955 is virtually a Kinsey document... At one point Kinsey is cited six times in twelve pages."⁵ In 1954, Hardy reports, after reviewing "a list of the council of the American Law Institute," Kinsey marked in red the name of Judge Hand, suggesting Hand "would probably support Kinsey's attempts to change the sex laws."⁶ In the end, the new code's sex law reform was largely based on Kinsey's "data" and would undermine the protections for marriage, then the only lawful place for coitus, consensual or not.

After a "grant from the Carnegie Corporation in 1948" aided the ALI in establishing joint educational efforts with the ABA, the Rockefeller Foundation stepped in to aid Carnegie. Stanford University Law School professors Kaplan and Weisberg wrote in *Criminal Law* (1991):

In 1950, the infusion of a large grant from the Rockefeller Foundation stirred the model penal code project to life again. An advisory committee, made up of distinguished scholars in the field of criminal law was assembled by the American Law Institute. Wechsler was appointed chief reporter [author] of the enterprise, and Louis Schwartz, another eminent authority in the field, was named co-reporter [author].⁷

The ALI's claimed goal is found in its mission statement crafted in 1923 "to promote the clarification and simplification of the law," to better adapt law to contemporary social needs, to achieve agreement among lawyers on "the fundamental principles of the common law," and to correct the legal "uncertainty and... complexity." Kaplan and Weisberg support the ALI claim that there was a "general dissatisfaction with the administration of justice,"[8] although nowhere do these writers note that this dissatisfaction centered on the public desire for lighter enforcement of extant criminal laws. Stanford law professor, Gerald Gunther, said the ALI, "is the elite incarnation of the American legal establishment, a select group of leading practitioners, scholars, and judges committed to "the improvement of the law." Gunther notes that Judge Hand was an ALI founder, and held "major positions in it for the rest of his life."[9] The 1996 Annual Report proclaimed:

The Institute's reputation for objectivity is one of its most valuable assets. The respect accorded the Institute's texts depends in major part on that reputation. The Institute's reputation will suffer if an accusation is made with any colorable basis that Institute texts were crafted to aid the personal interests of the Institute's Reporters. If the accusation were justified, the Institute's reputation would suffer, justifiably.[10]

At the very time the ALI's Model Penal code was being developed, there was a growing public outcry for tightening, *not loosening*, what were called "sexual psychopath" laws.

Then, by 1950, under cover of the American Bar Association and funded by Carnegie and Rockefeller grants, the tiny cadre of American Law Institute-Model Penal Code authors did not "clarify" America's common law, but rather radically gutted its sex laws based on Kinsey's data. Kinsey would indeed impact the American justice system at-large by being cited as the "scientific" expert by both the authors of the four books and the MPC authors as supposedly proving that "sex offenders" were 95 percent of America's fathers and beloved male family members. The ALI authors demanded and facilitated "a downward revision" of sex offender penalties because Kinsey said reality was out-of-step with the law. This was all based on Kinsey's aberrant groups of criminals, homosexuals, pedophiles and the like which fortified the ALI's Model Penal Code. The revision led to the weakening and deconstruction of the 52 sex offender laws targeted for change, undermining marriage as the single legitimate source of all coitus.

These distinguished ALI-MPC authors hailed from august institutions and were leaders in their professions. They are culpable. They knew or should have known that Kinsey was a fraud. (The Rockefeller Foundation knew his "data" were fraudulent.) The ALI authors' actions and writings reveal a "colorable bias," thereby seriously compromising the work and reputations of the Model Penal Code's "Institute's Reporters."

After Kinsey's bogus data entered "the stream of the law" through the ALI-MPC draft on "Sex Offenses" in 1955, the Kinsey sexuality model became codified as "normal" in mainstream America. It was taught by many unsuspecting law professors in America's most prestigious law schools. If Kinsey's science is any indication of the reliability of the ALI-MPC, one can only wonder at the efficacy of the entire effort. One might summarize the process by quoting Judge Robert Bork, "The legal system has started to judge by [a libertarian] ideology, not law."[11]

For Sir William Blackstone, whose books and teachings on the common law were foundational to American law, and for America's founders, the law was "revealed" and thus "eternal." Recognizing the limitations of human observation and reason, their view of the law was not determined on the basis of the scientific method of the time.[12] However, as science embraced Darwin's evolutionary theory of a changing or unfolding universe, the evolutionary view of law was seen as "progressive." Thus, it began following the evolutionary stream of relativism. Relativism became "positive" law, which in the 20th Century became confused with "the rule of law."

The principle of "fixed" law gave way to a process of constant change. This departure from fixed legal principle was championed by such learned men as scientist Charles William Eliot. From 1869-1909, as president of Harvard,[13] Eliot sought to apply the Darwinian scientific method to education and legal study. It appears that only professors who accepted the evolutionary law view were welcome at Harvard Law School.

As a biology student at Harvard (1916-1920), Kinsey entered the stream of the elite academic world where the new religion of relativism and scientific evolution was firmly rooted. Kinsey learned about Jacque Loeb's "New Biology" and the possible transformation of the world that was said to be the scientist's right and responsibility. In time, Kinsey would, like Eliot before him, join law with science to transform America's "fixed" laws regarding sexual offenses. Kinsey provided the evolutionary "scientific" justification for the arguments of legal revolutionaries, pioneering the legalization of all sexual "outlets."

Since January 2000 several hundreds of laudatory citations to Kinsey's data have appeared in USA Law Review Journals. Their authors use Kinsey's "data" to continue shaping our laws on marriage, adultery, abortion, sexual "orientation," sodomy, housing, adoption, child custody, sex offense reductions, registration, education, "compulsory monogamy," counseling, obscenity, pornography, child hearsay, homosexual immutability, natural law, cyber-predators, the sex industry, anti-discrimination statutes, family in prisons, behavioral addictions, due process, informational privacy, civil justice, opportunistic bias crimes, hemophilic mandates for health care providers, Lawrence v TX, "Gays" in the Military, Transgender immigration, cohabitation, sex trafficking, econometric abortion analyses, sex torts, homosexual parenting, securities class actions, sexual psychopath law, indecency censorship, school safety for "gays", race and "gay" identity, cinematic psychological conceptions, personal v community, gay pornography, the first amendment, polygamy, global human rights protection, transgendered prisoners, a breach of vows, homophobia, sexism, states' rights, transgender health care, religious liberty, Title IX, Title VII, pedophiles and cyber-predators, unborn victims of violence act, federalism, Wechsler and the Model Penal Code, prostitution, teen oral sex felons, pro-life suppression, science identity, sexual harassment, etc.

LEVERAGE IN POLITICS

Following release of the *American Legal Institute-Model Penal Code* (ALI-MPC) in 1955, the marital and financial obligations of many husbands and wives to their spouses and children diminished. "No-fault divorce" de-stigmatized adultery, and the payment of alimony, which had hampered the potentially errant husband and father, was ridiculed as an old-fashioned anachronism of sexual repression and Puritanism.

Writing in *The Family in America* (January 2000), Bryce Christensen addressed some of the appalling societal consequences from "no fault divorce." One of these has been the often draconian laws to collect child support from alleged "deadbeat dads" and now increasingly from mothers. The U.S. Census Bureau reported that in 1950, 43 percent of children were at home with Mom while Dad worked full-time. By 1990, only 18 percent of American children had such a stable home.[14] Christensen observed the concern, regarding the recent "public consensus" about children reared without a father, the "poverty and deprivation of children in female-headed households." Turning to that massive increase in single moms and inevitable child poverty, Christensen writes:

America's policymakers have given little or no regard to the social ideal of wedlock. Though zealous to reduce the child poverty which parental divorce has caused, they have shrunk from the task of preventing divorce in the first place. Indeed, the policy-makers pushing for tougher measures to collect child support have generally acquiesced in the liberal no-fault divorce statutes, which helped to drive up the divorce rate in the first place...

Few Americans would dispute a father's obligation to provide for his children. Throughout American history, any man who bore the title father bore also the title of provider...

It was because of this perceived linkage between wedlock and a man's obligation to act as a provider that in the case of an out-of-wedlock pregnancy, the extended family and local community often pressured the responsible young man into a shotgun wedding. Marriage made the young man publicly take upon himself the duty to provide for the unborn child and its mother.[15]

The above title by Christenson centers on "fault-based divorce," noting that pre-Kinsey, the adulterous male or female spouse forfeited child custody, while dad supported his children in any case. Once "fault" was eliminated from custody proceedings, adulterous, promiscuous moms have retained custody of children while the wronged father continued to pay child support. On the other hand, based on their higher incomes, under "no-fault" divorce, felons—even convicted incestuous fathers—have gotten custody of their children, while mothers have actually lost custody of their children. This has placed children in dire situations. Christensen is incredulous:

For unlike traditional divorce statutes, no-fault divorce undermines rather than reinforces marriage as a social ideal... no-fault divorce trivializes marriage, making it weaker than the weakest of contracts-at-will. It is now easier to dispose of an unwanted spouse of twenty years than to fire an unwanted employee of one year... Thomas B. Marvell calculated in 1989 that the adoption of no-fault statutes had driven up state divorce rates "by some 20 to 25 percent." And in a 1999 analysis, a team of statisticians determined that in the 32 states which had enacted no-fault laws by 1974, these laws "resulted in a substantial number of divorces that would not have occurred otherwise... Undermining marriage as a social ideal was not one of the objectives identified by the activists who pushed no-fault statues through in the 1960's and 1970's. Indeed, many of these activists claimed that their legal innovation would actually strengthen wedlock by helping men and women trapped in bad marriages to move into good marriages... [But] casual divorce has actually made men and women less likely to "commit fully" to a marital union, thus reducing the likelihood of marital success...

****

It is largely because no-fault has weakened the economic status of victimized former wives that feminist Betty Friedan, formerly a supporter, now admits, "I think we made a mistake with no-fault divorce"...

Most of all, recognizing wedlock as a social ideal will compel the surrender of the dangerous illusion that the bureaucratic machinery, of child-support-collection can somehow obviate the need for the personal virtues that sustain marriage and family life. Once we have all surrendered this illusion, then we can—with T.S. Eliot—finally break out of the spells woven by politicians "dreaming of systems so perfect no one will need to be good."[16]

"No-fault" divorce encouraged crime. The ALI-MPC role in encouraging fornication and adultery demoralized marriage and families and harmed millions of women and children financially, morally and physically. With "no-fault" divorce, women who had given their virginity, youth, dreams, labor and fidelity—their most significant "property" under common law—could be shabbily dismissed, their betrayal legally and socially trivialized. "No-fault" divorce swelled the ranks of "displaced homemakers," and their troubled and increasingly abandoned, dangerous children.

If, as Kinsey claimed, almost *everyone* engaged in pre-marital sex, then virginity was not a practiced virtue. Hence, condemnation of the crimes of seduction, fornication, cohabitation and adultery became antiquated and the ability to maintain a stable marriage and family for the individual and society significantly weakened.

LEVERAGE IN THE EDUCATIONAL SYSTEMS AT ALL LEVELS

Fortunately, Kinsey's findings were *not* duplicated in the work of Drs. Phyllis and Eberhard Kronhausen, the sexually radical couple[17] who recall also worked to free the world from sexual repression. Their "erotic" museum in Holland and, in an effort to further Kinsey's cause, conducted a sex survey of 200 male college students which they reported in their book *Sex Histories of American College Men* (1960).

The embarrassing secret of the sexual libertarians was that as much as the Kronhausens wanted to justify Kinsey's claims of widespread sexual promiscuity among college males, they were unable even by 1960 to locate such activity on campus.

The Kinsey team argued in 1948 and 1953 that sex education was needed to decrease sexual inhibition and increase orgasm, thereby enhancing marriages.

Cultural Power

Current sex education programs focus even on elementary school children, in part to help them prepare to avoid venereal diseases. During the Kinsey era, the only STDs commonly experienced were syphilis and gonorrhea. Today, after 50 years of Kinseyite conditioning, we can add to the list genital herpes, chlamydia, pelvic inflammatory disease (PID), bacterial vaginosis, trichomoniasis, hepatitis (A, B and C), cervical cancer, and many other maladies.

There was a 30 percent increase in reports of syphilis from 1985-1987, and about two million new cases of gonorrhea are reported annually. At least a quarter of the homosexual population is reportedly afflicted with gonorrhea of the tonsils. Chlamydia-related health costs are running around $1.3 billion annually; genital herpes reportedly afflicts about 25 million Americans; cervical cancer and genital warts are estimated at 12 million or so cases nationally; there are around 200,000 new cases of hepatitis B annually; and on and on.[18]

Kinsey's philosophy of early childhood sexual development became the standard for today's graphic sex instruction materials in many, if not most, American public, private, and parochial schools, usually camouflaged by such euphemistic captions as sex education, AIDS prevention or awareness, bullying prevention, gender respect, suicide prevention, family life, health, hygiene, home economics, physical education, even "abstinence" education.[18] New 'helpful' programs appear almost daily. Public health data confirm that as Kinseyan-based sex education has metastasized, levels of sexual disease and dysfunction have rocketed upward.

In fact, however, Kinsey's devious and deviant data has "opened up" children to precocious early sex activity (encouraged by pornography in our homes, schools and libraries), based on Kinsey's widely repeated and wholly unproven mantra that children are sexual from birth. These data from child rapists now influence our courts, education, medicine, theology, and politics, generating laws which violate parental rights to protect their children while undermining our culture in ways too numerous to count. Yet "accredited" AIDS and sex education in elementary, secondary, college, graduate, and post-graduate schools is almost entirely predicated on the Kinsey- an "variant" sex model.

In 1948, the Kinsey model began to permeate the educational establishment. It would indoctrinate doctors, teachers, ministers, social workers, attorneys, the military, and United States Supreme Court Justices.

In 1964, an accredited sexology degree became available from the New York University Health Department's School of Education, under youthful homosexual activist Deryck Calderwood, who died of AIDS. In 1978, the University of Pennsylvania, Department of Health's School of Education began offering similar Kinseyan New Biology training and degrees, directed by homosexual advocate Kenneth George.

As of this writing, the Institute for the Advanced Study of Human Sexuality offers a doctorate of education, four graduate programs, and seven basic credentials (including a "Safe Sex Certificate") which can be obtained swiftly with little or no prior training. These degrees are phony of course, and not ever recognized by <u>ANY</u> higher education institution or authority. Pomeroy, the Institute's then-academic dean, acknowledged that advanced sex degree applicants are accepted "off the street," provided that they do not have traditional preconceptions about sexual mores. The demand for Kinseyan-only standards is evident in the Institute's codified "Basic Sexual Rights" ethical oath, which legitimizes the Kinsey New Biology model of "consensual" adult-child sex, incest, child prostitution, and child pornography.

Under the guise of AIDS education, this profession has become even more aggressive in modeling its variant-sexuality standard for our nation's schoolchildren. For example, the late Deryck Calderwood, a onetime Society for the Scientific Study of Sex (SSSS) president who headed New York University's School of Education Sexuality Department, created a curriculum for middle-school children (subsequently a film-strip and video) entitled, *About Your Sexuality,* which graphically glamorized unprotected homosexual and heterosexual anal sodomy. As noted in the *New York Tribune*, Calderwood, who died young of AIDS, was "a disciple of sex pioneer Alfred Kinsey (who) believed, with Kinsey, no type of sexual behavior is abnormal or pathological."

In 1991, the Sex Information and Education Council of the United States (SIECUS) launched its series of "Guidelines for Comprehensive Sexuality Education." The guidelines were aimed at institutionalizing Kinseyan sexuality nationwide and influencing legislation dealing with sexuality issues. SIECUS claimed they would "provide accurate information about human sexuality." Building on a virtual sex education monopoly, only Kinseyan-trained teachers would be permitted in American schoolrooms (K-12) to develop "sexuality literacy:"

Sexuality education should only be taught by specially trained teachers. Professionals responsible for sexuality education must receive specialized training in human sexuality, including the philosophy and methodology of sexuality education. Ideally, teachers should graduate from academic courses or programs in schools of higher education that provide the professional with the most time-intensive and rich training. At a minimum, teachers should participate in extensive in-service courses, continuing education classes, or intensive seminars.[20]

What "human sexuality information" has SIECUS provided to children, parents, school boards, teachers, doctors, nurses, clergy, psychologists, social workers and the general culture?[21] In full agreement with the Kinsey Model, the organization suggested,

A partial list of safe sex practices for teens could include... massaging caressing, undressing each other, masturbation alone, masturbation in front of a partner, mutual masturbation... By helping teens explore the full range of safe sexual behaviors, we may help to raise a genera- tion of adults that do not equate sex with intercourse, or intercourse with vaginal orgasm, as the goal of sex.[22]

Nowhere in this "expert advice" does SIECUS mention marriage, or indicate that it should play a part—much less a central part—in the sexual scheme of things. Nowhere does it caution that the suggested activities might undermine love and trust, not to mention mental and physical health. Like Kinsey, SIECUS discourages "intercourse as the goal of sex," instead offering youngsters masturbatory activity with erotic entertainment (endorsed in their 1991 Guidelines as "erotic literature" and art"). In 1992, SIECUS produced a pamphlet, "Talk about Sex," which urged children not to reject the sexually exploitive media that surrounds them, but to "use" it as a sexual aid:

When talking to a friend or a possible sex partner, speak clearly... Movies, music and TV... often have a message about sexuality and can help possible sexual partners express their affection and sexual interest... Use entertainment to help talk about sexuality, TV, music videos... magazines are a good way to begin to talk about sexuality...[23]

Theses sexologists have stealthfully lobbied all states except two to allow "obscenity exceptions" for schools so that teachers can use obscene material with the youngest of children! Inspired by Kinsey, the *SIECUS Report* (1996) urged the use of "sexually explicit visual, printed or on-line materials" for schoolchildren in order to "reduce ignorance and confusion" and to help the children develop "a wholesome concept of sexuality." The official SIECUS position equates sodomy with marital sex as "any type of unprotected sexual intercourse (oral, anal or vaginal)."

Few people realize that the great library collection of... the Kinsey Institute... was formed very specifically with one major field omitted: sex education. This was because it seemed appropriate, not only to the Institute but to its major funding source, the National Institute of Mental Health, to leave this area for SIECUS to fill. Thus we applied and were approved for a highly important grant from the National Institute for Mental Health that was designed to implement a planned role for SIECUS to become the primary data base for the area of education [indoctrination] for sexuality."[24]

The SIECUS Sex Education Curriculum Board was also led by Pomeroy, Bell, Calderwood, Calderone, and McIlvenna—all Kinseyans and all committed to Kinsey's research findings, deviant standards and pedophile promotions.

Were Kinsey, Hirschfeld, Crowley, and Guyon alive today, (or for that matter, those of the Marxist "Frankfort school" including the USA college guru, Herbert Marcuse) they would no doubt be delighted to find their model of sex education dominating the media, the arts, and permeating most of our schools.

They would find their sexual model, "The Kinsey Model," embedded in laws and government policies. These sexual liberators and libertines would be pleased to see obscenity in corner drugstores, on the Internet, in public libraries, private and public schoolrooms and on roadside billboards.

LEVERAGE IN THE MEDIA

But how did Kinsey become an astute public relations wizard? An indication of the answer is found in the record of the Rockefeller Foundation's extensive influence on mass communication. During the late 1930s, writes Christopher Simpson in *Science of Coercion*, the Foundation "believed mass media... constituted a uniquely powerful force in modern society" for imposing the will of the elite "on the masses."[25] According to Simpson, "secret psychological war projects" to control public opinion were supported by America's tax-exempt foundations. For example, campaigns were developed to induce Americans to support U.S. entry into World War II. The Rockefeller Foundation funded communications experts from the field of social science to shape pre- and postwar public attitudes. In the postwar era, this experienced group of operatives turned its attention to our domestic population. Simpson continues:

[There was] a remarkably tight circle of men and women who shared several important conceptions about mass communication research. They regarded mass communication as a tool for social management and as a weapon in social conflict, and they expressed common assumptions concerning the usefulness of quantitative research-particularly experimental and quasi-experimental effects research, opinion surveys, and quantitative content analysis as a means of illuminating what communication "is" and improving its application to social management.[26]

Kinsey's quantitative research and numbers were a perfect fit with the Rockefeller plan to manipulate the mass media to "shape public attitudes and conduct." Such "social management" meant nothing less than changing America's way of life by altering what Kinsey called "breeding patterns" to conform to an animalistic, (pseudo-evolutionary) view of human sexual conduct as gall-wasps.

Simpson describes how agents trained in psychological warfare by the American intelligence and espionage apparatus (i.e., the Office of Strategic Services (OSS), forerunner of the Central Intelligence Agency (CIA), and the Office of War Information (OWI)) were infiltrated, with assistance from tax-exempt foundations, into influential positions in journalism, politics, university communications departments, and other powerful mass-media positions. There they could work to "engineer mass consent" as described by Christopher Simpson (addressed further in Chapter 10), and Simpson further states:

In 1939 the [Rockefeller] Foundation organized a series of secret seminars with men it regarded as leading communication scholars, to enlist them in an effort to consolidate public opinion in the United States in favor of war against Nazi Germany-opposed by many conservatives, religious leaders, and liberals at the time.[27]

[These secret psychological warfare projects] helped define U.S. social science and mass communication studies long after the war had drawn to a close. Virtually all of the scientific community that was to emerge during the 1950s as leaders in the field of mass communication research spent the war years performing applied studies on U.S. and foreign propaganda public opinion (both domestically and internationally), clandestine OSS operations.

Among OWI alumni-in 1953, are,

The publishers of *Time, Look, Fortune* and several dailies; editors of such magazines as *Holiday, Coronet, Parade,* and the *Saturday Review,* editors of The *Denver Post,* New Orleans' The *Times-Picayune,* and others; the heads of the Viking Press, Harper & Brothers, and Farrar, Straus and Young; two Hollywood Oscar winners; a two-time Pulitzer Prize winner; the board chairman of CBS and a dozen key network executives; President Eisenhower's chief speech writer; the editor of *Reader's Digest* international editions; at least six partners of large advertising agencies; and a dozen noted social scientists; chief of the U.S. government's covert psychological warfare effort from 1950 to 1952 and later dean of the Columbia Graduate School of Journalism and founder of the *Columbia Journalism Review*.

World War II psychological warfare work established social networks that opened doors to crucial postwar contacts inside the government, funding agencies, and professional circles [and] *unprecedented access to human research subjects*.[28] [Emphasis added.]

With connections to the mass media via the Rockefeller organization, Kinsey was able to generate widespread public curiosity and interest in his book prior to publication. And selection of the prestigious medical publisher W.B. Saunders served to further enhance the impression that the book was an authentic scientific endeavour.

LEVERAGE BY THE ENTERTAINMENT INDUSTRY

Not until a decade of *Playboy* (which was launched December 1953), and indoctrination of the pertinent professions (education, psychiatry, psychology, health, law, and the mass communications and entertainment media) with Kinseyan sexuality training, did a dramatically changed societal attitude begin to take place.

Although this book does not scrutinize the *Playboy* phenomenon in depth, two earlier works by Dr. Judith Reisman (*"Soft Porn" Plays Hardball,* (1991) and *Images of Children, Crime and Violence in Playboy, Penthouse and Hustler* (1989)) resulted from a U.S. Department of Justice (Office of Juvenile Justice and Delinquency Prevention) grant to study the causes of sex crimes by and against children. Both document the role of the named magazines (and pornography in general) in promoting and normalizing the Kinseyan "anything goes" view of human sexuality, including child sex abuse and incest.

As stated before, the fact that Kinsey was the cradle of the *Playboy* philosophy was confirmed by publisher Hugh Hefner, who reported during a 1996 BBC telecast that Kinsey was the researcher, but "I" was his "pamphleteer." The budding *Playboy* empire provided early and generous financial support for the Kinsey Institute.

During five decades of saturation with the Kinsey-Hefner view of human sexuality, America has witnessed a significant and disturbing change in the conduct of men and boys in general. Their addiction to pornography is causing a profound disintegration of our culture. Kinsey's misleading data have helped justify the "Me" generation and the general lowering of the status of women from helpmates to playmates. No longer divided into "virgins or whores," girls and women have increasingly become defined as "whores" in terms of their expected sexual conduct, and they and their children treated accordingly, undermining the moral order on which our nation was founded - our laws, institutions, and social attitudes. The accompanying erosion of the role of fathers has cost the nation dearly.

In June, 1999, the Washington, DC-based National Center for Public Policy Research (NCPPR) released a report which noted that "72 percent of Americans believe that fatherlessness is the most significant family or social problem facing America." Figures cited in the report paint a disturbing picture of the post-Kinsey view of fatherhood. For instance:

- Forty percent of the children of divorced parents haven't seen their dads in the past year.
- Thirty-six percent of children, approximately 24.7 million, don't live with their biological father. In 1960, just nine percent of children lived with only one parent.
- The number of live births to unmarried women increased from 224,300 in 1960 to 1,248,000 in 1995, while the

> number of children living with never married mothers grew from 221,000 in 1960 to 5,862,000 in 1995.
- National Fatherhood Initiative analysis found that of the 102 prime-time network TV shows in late 1998, only fifteen featured a father as a central character. Of these, the majority portrayed the father as uninvolved, incompetent or both. 29

In his biography of Kinsey, James Jones states:

In the consensus-minded 1950s, the mothers in television family programs such as *Ozzie and Harriet, Leave It To Beaver, Father Knows Best,* and *I Love Lucy* captured the officially sanctioned image of women. Fearful that Kinsey would reveal a contradiction between fictional women and real ones, many Americans did not want to hear what he had to say.[30]

Jones ignores the fact that the "officially sanctioned" image of women was significantly less fictional that what Kinsey "had to say."

The image of men and of fatherhood captured by pre-Kinsey television programs, scripted. Fathers largely working hard for their families, faithful to their wives, spending guiding and teaching time with their children, and playing an active role in their churches, communities, and schools. This was indeed the era of "Father knows Best," and it turns out that while this model of father did have its downside, it certainly had its upside, for the solvency of us all.

The NCPPR report observed that "for the kids who have them, a good dad makes a big difference." It cited as examples:

- Children with fathers are twice as likely to stay in school.

- Boys with dad and mom at home are half as likely to be incarcerated, regardless of their parent' income or educational level...
- Girls 15-19 raised in homes with fathers are significantly less likely to engage in premarital sex, and 76 percent of teenage girls surveyed said their fathers are very or somewhat influential over their decisions regarding sex.
- Girls raised in single-mother homes are more likely to give birth while single and are more likely to divorce and remarry...
- Paternal praise is associated with better behavior and achievement in school, while father absence increases vulnerability and aggressiveness in young children, particularly boys.
- Young children living without dads married to their moms are ten times as likely to be in poverty.
- Children living in households with fathers are less likely to suffer from emotional disorders and depression...
- A white teenage girl with an advantaged background is five times more likely to be a teen mom if she grows up in a household headed by a single mom instead of with her biological dad and mom.
- Children with involved dads are less susceptible to peer pressure, are more competent, more self-protective, more self-reliant and more ambitious.31

Our nation is experiencing an epidemic of criminal sexual conduct, a coarsening of society, loss of manners, multiple venereal diseases, adultery, homosexuality, anal sodomy, anonymous fornication, pornography, obsessive masturbation, rape, child sex abuse, and incest. A 1989 assessment by The National Research Council stated that Kinsey had "established, to some degree, social standards of what was acceptable common practice."[32] His crimes have indeed had consequences.

LEVERAGE BY THE PORNOGRAPHIC INDUSTRY

Writing in *The Pied Pipers of Sex,* Vernon Mark, a professor at Harvard Medical School, noted that the introduction of pornographic films into medical training, and the unwholesome influence of the films on individual doctors and the profession as a whole, were brought about by Kinsey. Physicians had traditionally been a highly respected class of spokesmen for sexual conservatism. Kinsey's obscenity training served to erode that standard.

As academic dean of the Institute for the Advanced Study of Human Sexuality (the cult that gives phony degrees and credentials to "sexperts"), Kinsey co-author Wardell Pomeroy sanctioned incest as beneficial when advising readers of *Penthouse, Chic,* and other pornographic magazines. He based his position on Kinsey Institute data supposedly supporting the notion of "positive incest."

The Sexual Attitude Restructuring (SAR) experience at The Institute for the Advanced Study of Human Sexuality (IASHS) has served as a critical tool to reshape views of human sexuality. The New Biology media, an orgy of pornographic couplings on film and video, is regularly utilized in academia to restructure students' modest sexual attitudes into the bizarre Kinseyan alternative. To understand how this works, it is useful to study the mechanics of the SAR in desensitizing and disinhibiting the human brain to allow a shift in pedagogical attitude and performance, especially since this is being done to third grade children today. The SAR literally scars the viewer's brain as it circumvents, short-circuits, his or her cognition and conscience. Neuroscientist Dr. Gary Lynch says of all high resonance stimuli: "What we're saying here is that an event which lasts half a second, within five or ten minutes has

Cultural Power

produced a structural change that is in some ways as profound as the structural changes one sees in (brain) damage."[33]

Revolutionary changes in the '90s have supported the continued liberalization of laws on sodomy, sex and reproduction. Based on the disproven assumption that sexual arousal can never be toxic, even laws against public nudity are often not enforced. In fact, the use of any age child in pornography, in sodomy, sadism and bestiality, was made legal in *New York v. Ferber* (1980) and unanimously reversed by the United States Supreme Court in 1982. The legitimizing of pedophilia lends support to the unrelenting efforts to legalize child pornography at the same time that children are widely exposed to pornographic stimuli in the mass media, schools and public libraries.

Few of the early pioneers working for uncensored media envisioned the current consequences, when children access obscenity by phone, Internet or in the school or public library. And few child advocates understand the role mainstream erotica/pornography has played in legitimizing, marketing and supplying child pornography. This author's study for the United States Department of Justice, Juvenile Justice and Delinquency Prevention, *Images of Children, Crime and Violence in Playboy, Penthouse and Hustler*, (1989) established that link. Even now child pornography can be ordered from *Playboy's* earlier editions and from other mainstream pornographic magazines as well as via the *Playboy Press* productions.[34]

The most notable mainstreaming of child pornography may still be the infamous 1976 *Playboy Press* pictures of the then 7-year-old child, Brooke Shields, in *Sugar and Spice, Surprising and Sensuous Images of Women*. *Playboy Press* posed a naked, oiled Brooke Shields in the context of other sadistic, pseudo-lesbian and racist pornography. All would "stir the sex impulses or... lead to sexually impure and lustful thoughts" (thought being the neurochemical "action" changing the brain structure).[35]

The Kinsey Institute and Indiana University played a major role in deliberately, undermining, and eventually overturning America's obscenity laws, allowing obscenity to be used teaching tool for primary school children!. The Institute pornography was shown and explained in 1970 to the President's Commission on Pornography, bolstering the Commission's Kinseyan conclusions about the harmlessness and usefulness of pornography for children and society.[36]

Kinsey would be thrilled by the extent to which "The Kinsey Model" was entrenched everywhere, the way non-marital sex, adultery, sodomy, and bi/homosexuality are glamorized in film and on TV. He would delight in watching teachers instruct grade-school children on how to place condoms on bananas, cucumbers, and wooden penises, and how to make models of their sex organs in Play-Doh. And he would thrill at the sight of schoolrooms plastered with sexual and patently pornographic AIDS posters, while the Ten Commandments are prohibited by judge-made "law."

No other 20th Century figure can equal Alfred C. Kinsey for achieving widespread public acceptance of the disordered and destructive elements of his own troubled imagination, or in wreaking havoc on our culture in the name of "science."

CHAPTER 3 NOTES

1. *International Encyclopedia of the Social Sciences*, 1968, p. 389.
2. Cochran, Mosteller, Tukey and Jenkins, *Statistical Problems of the Kinsey Report; A Report of the American Statistical Association Committee to Advise the National Research Council Committee for Research in Problems of Sex*, The American Statistical Association, Washington, DC, 1954.
3. C.F. Turner, H.G. Miller and L.E. Moses, Eds. *AIDS, Sexual Behavior and Intravenous Drug Use*, National Research Council, National Academy Press, Washington, D.C., 1989, p. 79.

4. Brandeis' concern about the subversive nature of "philanthropies" is found in Rene Wormser, *Foundations: Their Power and Influence*, Covenant House, Sevierville, Tennessee, 1993, p. 6.

5. Christopher Simpson, *Science of Coercion: Communication Research & Psychological Warfare* 1945-1960, Oxford University Press, New York, 1994, pp. 29-31. Eugenicists would close the book on the "fixed" view of human life, that is, the view of man and woman as in the image of God, as His agents, producing–within a protective and prescribed marital act–their own offspring and conferring to them "life, liberty and the pursuit of happiness," fundamental to the American way of life. Eugenicists bring the ancient theology to America. So while science was the method, religion was the aim.

Man in control and moving irreversibly closer to the *Brave New World is* detailed in Aldous Huxley's "fiction" where the words "mother and father" are obscenities; family's non-existent; adults totally promiscuous never marrying; and private property non-existent. Con- trolled offspring are produced in efficient state-run hatchery laboratories, "decanted" from test tubes, and raised in state sponsored institutions where they are encouraged to engage in "erotic play" on the playground. When depression and the meaninglessness of this life overwhelm them, the inhabitants self-medicate at will using "soma," a drug to enhance and relax or to relieve anxiety or any cowardly reaction to their existence in the "brave new world." The Rockefeller agencies appear to be working toward a similar eugenic world for American law, medicine, social sciences, mass communications, and government, while neutralizing the Church and the ministry as effective representatives of the Creator's fixed order.

6. Kinsey, on "Reputations," *Biography*, BBC-TV, rebroadcast on Arts & Entertainment, 1996.

7. Plutocracy is defined as government by a wealthy class, Encarta, 1997.

4. *This is ALI-ABA*. Brochure, unpaginated, The American Law Institute, Philadelphia, Penn., October 18, 1995, p. 1.

5. Jonathan Gathorne-Hardy, *Sex, Alfred C. Kinsey, The Measure of All Things*, Chatto & Windus, London, 1998, p. 449.

6. Id., p. 158.

7. John Kaplan and Robert Weisberg, *Criminal Law, Cases and Materials, Second Edition*, Little, Brown and Company, Law Book Division, Boston, Mass., Appendix B, "A Note on the Model Penal Code", 1991, pp. 1165-1168.

8. *This is the American Law Institute*, Rev. Brochure, unpaginated, The American Law Institute, Philadelphia, July 1995, p. 1.

9. Gerald Gunther, *Learned Hand: The Man and the Judge*, Alfred A. Knopf, New York, 1994, p. 410.

10. The American Law Institute Annual Reports, May 14-17, Washington, D.C., 1996, p. 19.

11 Quote from speech by Judge Bork, cited in Barbara Olson, *Hell To Pay*, Regnery Publishing, Washington, D.C., 1999, p. 52.

12. Herbert W. Titus, *God, Man and Law: The Biblical Principles,* Institute in Basic Life Principles, Oak Brook, Illinois, 1994, p. 5.

13. Id., p. 2.

14. *USA Snapshots*, December 27, 1999.

15. Bryce Christensen, "Deadbeat Dads," in *The Family in America,* January 2000, pp. 1-7.

16. Id.

17. *Male*, p. 153.

18. See Reisman, *et al, Kinsey, Sex and Fraud: The Indoctrination Of A People, Huntington House, Lafayette, LA, 1990, pp. 92-100 for a brief summary of current data on these venereal diseases.*

19. SIECUS, *Sexuality in Man,* Scribners, New York, 1970, pp. 6-7.

20. SIECUS "Guidelines for Comprehensive Sexuality Education, the National Guidelines Task Force, 1991, p. 9.

21. See *Time* magazine article citing this issue of SIECUS ("Attacking the Last Taboo," April 14, 1980) for a discussion of "sex research- ers" promoting incest.

22. "Safe Sex and Teens," by Debra W. Haffner, *SIECUS Report*, September/October 1988, p. 9.

23. SIECUS, "Talk About Sex," 1992.

24. Mary Calderone, writing about SIECUS' role in promoting Kinsey's message, *SIECUS* Report, May-July 1982, p. 6.

25. Christopher Simpson, *Science of Coercion: Communication Research & Psychological Warfare*, 1945-1960, Oxford University Press, New York, 1994, p. 29.

26. Simpson, pp. 20-22 and 29.

27. Christopher Simpson, *Science of Coercion: Communication Research & Psychological Warfare*, 1945-1960, Oxford University Press, New York, 1994, pp. 22-23.
28. Simpson, pp. 28-30
29. Drs. Phyllis and Eberhard Kronhausen, *Sex Histories of American College Men,* Ballantine Books, New York, 1960, p. 15.
30. Amy Ridenour, "Be Thankful for Dads," National Policy Analysis #252, National Center for Public Policy Research Analysis, June, 1999.
31. James Jones, *Alfred C. Kinsey; A Public/Private Life*, W.W. Norton, New York, 1997, p. 679.
32. Ridenour, op cit.
33. T*he Brain: Learning and Memory*, The Annenberg CPB Collection, Santa Barbara, CA., WNET, 1984.
34. Back issues of *Playboy* and other pornographic magazines can be purchased using the toll free numbers for these materials. This author has obtained what was illegal "child pornography" from said agents.
35. Judith Reisman, *"SoftPorn" Plays Hard Ball*, Huntington House, Lafayette, LA, 1990, p. 36-37, citing Thomas Weyr, *Reaching for Paradise*, Times Books, New York, 1978, p. 105
36. See the Indiana University Kinsey Institute brochures describing the visits by the Pornography Commission to their facilities. The Kinsey Institute brochure distributed during the 1980s under "Services," states "Members of the Institute have been in great demand to deliver lectures, serve on panels, and act as consultants. In many instances individuals and groups visit the Institute to confer and obtain information, such as the congressionally appointed Committee on Obscenity and Pornography (page numbers unreadable).

CHAPTER 4

ORGANIZATIONAL POWER

The Kinsey Institute, Planned Parenthood, and the America Civil Liberties Union are a modern axis of evil, united in their relentless opposition to God as revealed in Judeo-Christian Scriptures.

Dr. Lloyd H. Stebbins

LEVERAGE BY THE ONGOING KINSEY INSTITUTE

The Kinsey Institute began its live obscenity productions prior to publication of the 1948 *Male* volume. Kinsey received Rockefeller monies for his "library" activities in 1946. Just as Kinsey "paid Martin out of his own pocket" until 1941, so too did he apparently pay photographer William Dallenback personally until the Rockefeller funds arrived. Then both men appear to have become "permanent member[s] of the Institute staff," and expensive film equipment was purchased.[1] It is likely that some of the Rockefeller largesse was earmarked for the pornographic productions. After all, they were a passion which Kinsey eagerly shared with visiting "scholars" from the Foundation, whom James Jones asserts became "hooked" on Kinsey.[2] Moreover, in his May 7, 1951 letter to "CIB," Warren Weaver complains that Kinsey's "library of erotic literature, and a collection of pictures and other 'art' objects of erotic significance" were essentially funded by Rockefeller.

Writing in 1951, Weaver recalled his 1946 objection to the funding of Kinsey's "erotica:"

> The latter phase has become sufficiently important so that they have installed and equipped a complete photographic laboratory, and have a full-time photographer who receives $4,800 per year... This library was started with the aid of a grant, additional to his then general support, made directly from the RF to Kinsey and for the specified purpose. As a matter of record, I remind you that I opposed that grant when it was discussed in officers' conference. Now this library-art aspect of their work surely requires, out of his total general budget... more than the total annual amount the RF is contributing. I contend that *it is perfectly realistic to say that the RF is paying for this collection of erotica and for the activities directly associated with it.* And I say further that I don't think we need to, or ought to [Emphasis added.][3]

After Kinsey died in 1956, Paul Gebhard became head of the Institute for Sex Research, while Wardell Pomeroy moved on to The Sex and Drug Forum, which later evolved into the Institute for the Advanced Study of Human Sexuality (IASHS). Although it has never been approved by any degree granting institution, it is now the leader in the sexology field (controlling conference selections, journal publications, lectures, etc.). IASHS has trained more than 100,000 sex educators, doctors, and "safe sex" instructors. It is a Kinseyan filter through which almost all "accredited" persons in the sexuality field are screened at some point during their careers. The more formal course work includes such topics as "erotic sensate and massage therapy," including sexual films; how to use surrogates (prostitutes) in sex therapy; analysis of the Kinsey reports; how to create "sex-education curricula"; child sexuality (taught by Dr. Pomeroy); "forensic sexology"; and teaching students how to give expert-witness court testimony favoring obscenity, pornography, and reduced penalties for sex crimes. None of these "sexperts" can be recognized as authorities now.

> As academic dean at the IASHS, Pomeroy also required staff members to participate in a variety of sex acts to break down their inhibitions and ensure that his team would be comprised of true-believing Kinseyans.

Kinsey's aggressive, intrusive, and arguably illegal conduct was protected by Indiana University's public relations apparatus. We now know that some of the women and children in publicity photographs may have paid a high price to maintain the carefully honed Kinsey image. Many officials and scholars covered up Kinsey's highly improper activities during his lifetime, and continue to do so at the Kinsey Institute and Indiana University today.

Also revealing is the portrayal of obscenity in the October, 1997, issue of the Kinsey Institute publication, *Kinsey Today*. A pornographic exhibition ("The Art of Desire") was announced as part of a pending celebration of the 50th anniversary of the initial Kinsey report:

> While the anniversary exhibition is a testament to the power and pervasiveness of human sexual expression... events surrounding the exhibition also attest to the persistence of fear of knowledge of sexuality. The Art of Desire opened on the evening of a protest on the Bloomington town square by the Concerned Women of America, one in a series of demonstrations across the country calling for the closure of the Kinsey Institute. Their objective appears to be to discredit Alfred Kinsey, and, in the process, to undermine and eventually eliminate sex education in public schools. Their overarching charge is that Kinsey is responsible for a decline in sexual morals and in the importance of the

> family in American society... Surely others had the training, the research background, the ability to ask the sometimes frightening questions Alfred Kinsey asked us about ourselves... Yet only he dared.[4]

In the same issue, the editors of *Kinsey Today* complained that their collection of 75,000 prints, 218 amateur albums, and 1,732 vintage negatives depicting aspects of human sexuality is "deteriorating."

> [Hence the Institute needs public] funding from the National Endowment for the Humanities (NEH)... to catalog and process these collections... to build an automation database that will have finding AIDS with brief, item-level entries.

In the same way that America refurbished and maintains at public expense, say, President Abraham Lincoln's boyhood home, the Kinsey Institute apparently believes that Alfred Kinsey's "free love" library also qualifies as a national treasure worthy of restoration and upkeep at taxpayers' expense. It is somewhat ironic that Lincoln signed a law on March 3, 1865, which outlawed obscenity[5] within the United States.[6] And years earlier, he warned during an address at Springfield, Illinois (January 27, 1838): "If destruction be our lot we must ourselves be its author and finisher. As a nation of freemen we must live through all time, or die by suicide."[7]

LEVERAGE BY PLANNED PARENTHOOD

In 1964, the Sex Information and Education Council of the United States (SIECUS) was launched at the Kinsey Institute. Its objective was to teach Kinseyan ideology as sex education in our schools. SIECUS (which now calls itself the *Sexuality* Information and Education Council of the United States) imprinted the new Kinsey variant standard on almost all sex education curricula. Its early leader, Dr. Mary Calderone (past medical director of Planned Parenthood) was the direct link between Kinsey's university-based research, Planned Parenthood's grassroots outreach, and SIECUS. SIECUS was a "Resource Center [operating] Specialized Programs to Distribute Information about Human sexuality [through] learned journals, research studies, training materials for health professionals and sample classroom curricula."[8]

Planned Parenthood (PP) has a history as fraught with special interests as has SIECUS and scores of books have been written about its movement into the schools, carrying the SIECUS banner of pseudo-science. PP was given a boost by Kinsey's claims that children are sexual and that "normal" women commonly have sex prior to marriage. Kinsey also urged that abortion be legalized, based on his wholly spurious data on the commonality of abortion in the USA, and in April 1955 he delivered a preliminary report on his abortion data at a PP abortion conference at Columbia University's Arden House which became a foundation for the pro-abortion movement.[9] A Planned Parenthood booklet given by teachers to secondary level schoolchildren, entitled "You've Changed the Combination!!!" was decorated with illustrations of nude, *Playboy*-like, large-bosomed women towering over small, wimpy nude males. It recommended that children have sex—but only with their "friends." It also equated virginity with prostitution since some girls remained virgins until they married:

> Do you want a warm body? Buy one. That's right. There are women who have freely chosen that business, buy one... Do you want a virgin to marry? Buy one. There are girls in that business too. Marriage is the price you'll pay, and you'll get the virgin. Very temporarily.[10]

One of several other "special interest" associations whose economic and social base now includes "sexuality instruction" is the American Association of Marriage and Family Counselors. The current decisions by the American Psychiatric Association (1994) in its *Diagnostic and Statistical Manual IV* to remove pedophilia, masochism and sadism as mental or psychological disorders and a 1999 article in the *American Psychological Association Bulletin* which would normalize adult sex with "willing" children, means these two powerful mental health agencies have joined forces with Kinsey's other pedophile advocates.[11]

Virtually without exception, the basis of professional training is Kinsey's duplicitous data, and that of his disciples who have built upon the false foundation he established.

From the "informal" sex education reaching nearly all children via pornography, to the "formal" sex education from doctorate to kindergarten, the Kinsey Model is the monopoly. The foundation of the modern sex industry then, from sex commerce to the sex "expert" who serve as expert witnesses for pornographers, all stand on the legitimacy of wholly illegitimate pseudoscience. Next we will examine how this "education" process has been used to reshape our laws on sex offenses, to fit the Kinsey Model, impacting the lives of every American.

In their book, *Blessed are the Barren*, authors Marshall and Donovan reference the famous Kinsey's Planned Parenthood speech,

> At the 1955 abortion conference sponsored by the Planned Parenthood Federation of America... the question of physician-induced abortion came up. The discussion leader on this point was the famed sex researcher, Alfred Kinsey.[12]

In 1965, the late Dr. Abraham Stone[13] and the late Dr. Norman Himes wrote *Planned Parenthood: A Practical Handbook of Birth-Control Methods*. The authors cite:

> The problem of induced abortion in the United States was covered in depth at the 1955 Arden House Conference on

Abortion sponsored by the Planned Parenthood Federation of America. *An attempt was made to determine the extent and size of the problem.* The late Dr. Alfred C. Kinsey reported to this conference the results obtained by *his group sampling methods.* Abortion data was gathered by the Kinsey group as part of the total record of female sexual activity; the sample reported consisted of 4,248 pregnancies occurring in 5,299 white females. The proportion of *premarital conceptions in this group terminated by induced abortion was in the range of 88 to 95 per cent! Of the married women in the sample, 22 per cent had at least one abortion of an unwanted pregnancy by age forty-five.* Among all the single women who had had coitus, the abortion incidence was 20 per cent.[14]

The attempt to show massive abortions—and the harmlessness of abortion—required that the Kinsey team find, as they did, that abortions were largely beneficial. They actually improved marriages, and were found safe and morally acceptable to the medical profession. But, to do so meant that almost all abortions had to be carried out by "physicians" with largely favorable results.[15] To accomplish this flight of fancy, the Kinsey team returned to their successful ploy of redefining the common English language—like that of "married" women—which inevitably misled and confused legislators, the public and other scholars, as well as judges and juries. The Gebhard abortion team reported:

> "Physicians" accounted for about 85 per cent of the abortions in our white non-prison sample, **although in some of these cases the "physician" did not have a medical license.** Although operative techniques were reported to have been used in over 90 per cent of our white non-prison sample, they were reported in only 72 per cent of the white prison sample...[16] [Emphasis added.]

So, the Gebhard team claims a "physician" (their quotes) is a physician even without a medical license (ignored in the pro-abortion debate). And, how many were "some physicians"? Were 50 percent, 75 percent, 90 percent, 99 percent, "some" without a license? The claim that most abortions were so uncomplicated and morally neutral that they were customarily performed illegally by medical doctors, got wide distribution via Planned Parenthood and SIECUS.

LEVERAGE BY AMERICAN CIVIL LIBERTIES UNION

American Sexual Behavior and the Kinsey Report was a very important contribution to the growing "free love" legal debate was co-authored by ACLU attorney, Morris L. Ernst, and historian David Loth. The book's dedication was to the accommodating Kinsey team who "enriched the market-place of thought."[17] Ernst advocated legalization of adultery, obscenity, and abortion throughout his career, as well as Kinsey's full panoply of sex law changes:

> Let me mention a few items on which law must say thank you [to Kinsey]. Our laws have attempted to abolish all sexual outlets, except marital intercourse... [including] sodomy [and] seduction... Forty-four states have laws against adultery. ...Yet the Kinsey report may well... show that one third of all husbands [commit adultery]...Those who are concerned with juvenile delinquency, treatment of homosexuals, and the frightening attitudes of our penal institutions will have a glimmer of what the Kinsey report will do to the stream of law.[18]

Ernst was influential. He served as a "personal representative for President Roosevelt during World War II."[19] Moreover, he was well credentialed as a legal radical for serving as a founding member of the American Civil Liberties Union (ACLU).[20] Ernst was also the attorney for Kinsey, Margaret Sanger (founder of Planned Parenthood), the Kinsey Institute, the Sex Information and Education Council of the United States (SIECUS), and Planned Parenthood of America. Ernst had close ties to influential and progressive Supreme Court Justices Louis Brandeis, Brennan, Frankfurter and Judge Learned Hand,[21] among others. Through the considerable efforts of Ernst, the Kinsey study would have special salience in the courtroom as its findings were plied there. That Ernst was Kinsey's lawyer[22] was hushed up. On the evidence, Ernst was a trusted Kinsey aide years before he admitted to knowing the zoologist. Upon analysis, Kinsey's law language dips deeply into that of the ACLU lawyer and the French pedophile judge, discussed further on. Kinsey's false data first entered, as Ernst said, in "the stream of the law" through the ALI-MPC, "Tentative Draft No. 4," dealing with "Sex Offenses," on April 25, 1955.

1948 Ernst & Loth Crimes List (52 Sex Sex Crimes for Civil Order) Targeted for Abolition or Lightening by the Kinsey Legal Cadre

Crimes against Nature
  a. Sodomy
  b. Bestiality
  c. Buggery
  d. Cunnilingus
  e. Fellatio
Adultery
Indecent Exposure
Disorderly Houses
Nuisance
Disorderly Conduct
Pornographic Literature
Immoral Shows and Exhibitions
Contraception – Indecent Articles
Bastardy
Bigamy
Chastity*
Lewd Cohabitation
Incest
Lewd Acts with Infants [oft defined as under 18-years-of-age]
Crimes Against Infants (Minors)
  a. Impairing morals of a minor
  b. Prostitution
  c. Abduction
  d. Seduction
  e. Statutory Rape
Abortion
Fornication
Contacts (Sexual Immorality)
Compulsory Prostitution of Wife

Transportation for Immoral Purpose
Nudist Camps
Abduction
Seduction
Prostitution
Rape
  a. By force
  b. Statutory
Lewd Behavior
Obscene Books, Letters, Communications
Assault with Intent to Commit Sodomy
Assault with Intent to Commit Rape
Solicitation with Intent to Commit Sodomy
Solicitation with Intent to Commit Prostitution
Illicit Intercourse
Publication of Sex Crimes Magazines
Advertisements Relating to Certain Diseases
Exposure of Person
Males Living on Proceeds of Prostitution
Sending Messages to Places of Prostitution
Allowing Children to Remain in Houses of Prostitution or Any Place Where Opium or Other Such Preparations is Smoked
Smoking Opium and Other Preparations
Concealing Birth of a Child
Libel of Sexual Behavior
Slander of Sexual Behavior
Compulsory Prostitution by Parents of Children (female and in some States, male)
Miscegenation
Obscene Language

*Here the authors include "chastity" as a sex crime. One assumes this "joke" was a reflection of the authors specific views.

Other drafts covering other areas of law followed. All found their way into legislation and judicial decisions. With the ALI-MPC drafts and the four books previously mentioned by such notable professionals and academics, the legal profession and state legislatures thereafter began to gradually ignore, lighten, or repeal the 52 sex-related crimes that Ernst and Loth had included in their book, *American Sexual Behavior and the Kinsey Reports*.[23] A "separate volume could be written about each statute in relation to the Kinsey data." [See following chart.] Standing on the notion of the alleged right of privacy, the Kinsey legal cadre judged the 52 protective laws as largely illegitimate. By accepting Kinsey's data, almost all sex acts would be "restated" as private and not subject to social control.

CHAPTER 4 NOTES

1. Wardell Pomeroy, *Dr. Kinsey and the Institute for Sex Research*, Harper & Row, New York, 1972, p. 87 and James H. Jones, *Kinsey, A Private/Public Life*, W. W. Norton, New York, 1997, p. 606-607.

2. James H. Jones, *The Origins of the Institute for Sex Research*, UMI Dissertation Services, Ann Arbor, Michigan, 1973, pp. 256, 259.

3. Warren Weaver letter to CIB, May 7, 1951, pp. 8-10, Rockefeller Center Archive.

4. *Kinsey Today*, Kinsey Institute for Research in Sex, Gender, and Reproduction, Fall 1997, Volume 1, Number 2.

5. *Kinsey Today*, p. 5.

6. Terrence J. Murphy, *Censorship, Government and Obscenity*, Helicon, Baltimore, Maryland, 1963, p. 75.

7. John Bartlett, *Familiar Quotations*, 14th Edition, [Ed.] Emily Morison Beck, Little, Brown and Company, 1968 [1855], p. 63

8. SIECUS brochure, "Are you going to stand by; will you?" undated, circa late 1980s.

9. Wardell Pomeroy, *Dr. Kinsey and the Institute for Sex Research*, Harper & Row, New York, 1972, p. 394.

10. Distributed by Planned Parenthood and published by Rocky Mountain Planned Parenthood, Colorado, 1974.

11. *Los Angeles Times* for July 19, 1999 published an article by libertarian Carol Travis entitled "Uproar Over Sexual Abuse Study Muddies the Waters." Travis writes: "I guess I should be reassured to know that Congress disapproves of pedophilia and the sexual abuse of children. On July 12, the House voted unanimously to denounce a study that the resolution's sponsor, Matt Salmon (R-Ariz.), called 'the emancipation proclamation of pedophiles. What got Congress riled was an article last year in the journal Psychological Bulletin, which is to behavioral science what the *Journal of the American Medical Assn.* is to medicine." The authors of that article-

-Bruce Rind, Philip Tromovitch and Robert Bauserman--concluded, from their meta-analysis of a non-random selection of 59 "studies" of child sexual abuse, that if the child is "willing," sex with an adult may be rewarding and harmless and that "non-judgmental" language should be used when referring to child molesters (i.e., terming sex with children "adult-child sex" rather than "child sexual abuse). Following the Congressional resolution and massive pressure from "Dr. Laura," the APA apologized and backed down from its publication of this pedophile promotional piece. Recent revelations that two of the three supposedly objective APA authors have ties with Paidika: The Journal of Paedophila raise serious questions about their objectivity. An article by Robert Buserman, entitled "Man-Boy Sexual Relationships in a Cross-Cultural Perspective," appeared in the Summer 1989 issue of *Paidika*. The Winter 1995 issue includes a book review by Bruce Rind, and recommends an article by Bauserman and Rind.

12. Robert Marshall and Charles Donovan, *Blessed are the Barren: The Social Policy of Planned Parenthood*, Ignatius Press, San Francisco, CA, 1991, p. 260.

13. Stone was also Director of the Margaret Sanger Research Bureau and Vice-President of the Planned Parenthood Federation of America, the International Planned Parenthood Federation, and the American Society for the Study of Sterility. Hines was an editor and con- tributor to the *Encyclopedia of the Social Sciences and the Encyclopedia Sexualis*.

14. Stone and Himes, *Planned Parenthood: A Practical Handbook of Birth-Control Methods,* Collier Books, New York, 1965, p. 235.

15 Gebhard, Pomeroy, Martin, Christenson, *Pregnancy, Birth and Abortion*, the "Science Editions", John Wiley & Sons, Inc., New York, 1958, pp. 205-206.

16. Id., p. 212.

17. Morris Ernst and David Loth, *American Sexual Behavior and The Kinsey Report*, Graystone Press, New York, 1948.

18. Morris Ernst, "The Kinsey Report and the Law," in *Sexual Behavior in American Society*, Jerome Himehach and Sylvia Fava, editors, W.W. Norton, New York, 1948, pp. 247-248.

19. Morris Ernst, *A Love Affair With The Law*, The MacMillan Company, New York, 1968, back cover.

20. Claire Chambers, *The SIECUS Circle*, Western Islands, Belmont, Massachusetts, 1977, p. 29.

21. Ronald D. Ray, "Kinsey's Legal Legacy," *The New American,* January 19, 1998, pp. 31-32.

22. Wardell Pomeroy, *Dr. Kinsey and the Institute for Sex Research*, Harper & Row, New York, 1972, p. 344.

23. Ernst and Loth, supra, n. 28, p. 127.

AMERICA
DARK SLIDE-BRIGHT FUTURE

PART III

PATH TO RECOVERY

CHAPTER 5
WHERE ARE WE TODAY? WHAT COMES NEXT?

Righteousness exalts a nation, but sin is a disgrace to any people.

Proverbs 14:34 NIV

For the wisdom of this world is foolishness with God...The Lord knoweth the thoughts of the wise, that they are vain.

1 Corinthians 3:19-20 KJV

When misguided public opinion honors what is despicable and despises what is honorable, punishes virtue and rewards vice, encourages what is harmful and discourages what is useful, applauds falsehood and smothers truth under indifference or insult, a nation turns its back on progress and can be restored only by the terrible lessons of catastrophe.

Frederic Bastiat, 19th Century French Political Economist

THE POWER OF KINSEY'S LONG-TERM IMPACT

Alfred Kinsey was the leader of massive efforts to destroy the American culture. He was a perverted, homosexual, pedophile. As an aggressive atheist, he despised the Bible, Judeo-Christian tradition, and all things religious. These were the biases that drove Kinsey's bogus research. Yet, his work has been financed by the Rockefeller Foundation and for 60 years has been trumpeted by the media, proclaimed by academics, gleefully promoted by politicians, popularized by Hollywood, and cited as reliable science in well over 5,796 scholarly law, social science, and scientific journals.

The American culture was infected by his findings first as the G.I. Bill pushed the Greatest Generation through the post-WWII universities and again when the wave of Baby Boomers attended. Kinsey's views were embedded in Hugh Hefner's Playboy Philosophy and largely contributed to the moral chaos in the 1960s and 70s. Today, the student leaders of that chaos occupy the highest levels of government. Kinsey opened the Kinsey Institute at Indiana University to sponsor and promote his views. Although he died in 1956, the Institute still exists. It has been supported by government funding for over 60 years and continues to pump out massive amounts of literature supporting all manner of sexual perversion masquerading as the sex education materials used throughout the American educational system. Kinsey was inducted into Legacy Walk in 2012; it is a public display celebrating LGBT history.

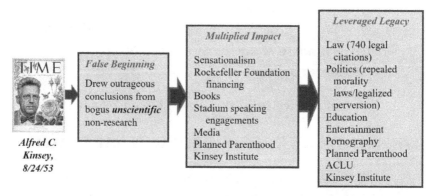

Alfred C. Kinsey, a Humanist savior, devastated the American culture.

Kinsey's big lie was based on bogus "research." Nevertheless, the impact of his personal work was multiplied by aggressive promotion, the titillating nature of sex. and a broad multidisciplinary array of personal contacts. He was even granted a particularly flattering cover of Time magazine on August 24, 1953. Although Kinsey died almost exactly three years later, on August 25, 1956, all manner of Humanist and Humanist organizations have, in the last 50 years, carried his banner and forcefully embedded Kinsey's philosophy throughout the American culture.

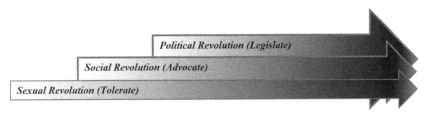

The sexual revolution spawned by Kinsey, triggered a social revolution, which promoted a political revolution.

In rapid succession, Kinsey created a sexual revolution, followed by a social revolution—responsible for the upheaval of the 1960s and 1970s—and finally the political revolution. All three continue today. The initial toleration of his perversions became acceptance, followed by advocacy, and ultimately legalization through the political and legal processes.

WHERE WERE THE JUDEO-CHRISTIAN BELIEVERS?

Where were the Judeo-Christian believers most likely to object to the Kinsey-initiated juggernaut? Did they simply hide under a rock or in their homes and places of worship? No—the pressures of political correctness did not arise until several decades after Kinsey's death. Believers slowly compromised to the point of near oblivion. Consider the process.

Before 1960, there was a comprehensive set of laws in every state prohibiting everything identified in the Bible as sin, i.e. doing something my way instead of God's way. Why? The American culture rested on three rock-solid anchors, the Bible, the Declaration of Independence/U.S. Constitution combination, and the God-created, God-designed impregnable family.

The strength of a culture emerges from the continuous interactions of the intellectual, emotional, and spiritual aspects of the culture. In the American culture, the Bible is the spiritual anchor—the ultimate anchor. It is known by many believers as the inspired, inerrant Word of God. The combination of the Declaration of Independence and the U. S. Constitution is the physical/intellectual anchor. It is the earthly embodiment of the Biblical message. The family, as God created and designed it is the emotional anchor. The three anchors are rock-solid. Anything that weakens any one or all of them is like whittling away at one or more legs of a three-legged stool. Eventually, the stool will fall. "A cord of three strands is not quickly broken." [*Ecclesiastes 4:12 NIV*]

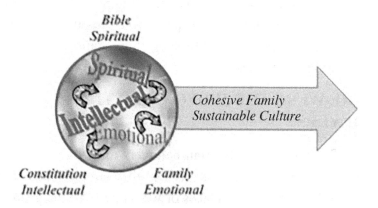

America's culture rests on three rock-solid anchors.

God identified certain thoughts and activities as sin, because they puff self and weaken the family. The family, as God designed it, is the only way to preserve a thriving human culture from generation to generation. The network of pre-1960 temporal laws prohibiting Biblical sin, guaranteed the integrity of the family.

Personal growth in godly character is a lifetime journey learning to value others before self. Such learning must begin early within the family as parents and children learn from each other as they face daily challenges that tend to reinforce prideful self at the expense of others. If people do not learn to exercise self-restraint and value others before self, within the family, they are unlikely to learn it anywhere else. In the absence of collective, cultural self-restraint, a culture or country declines rapidly into chaos and self-destruction.

However, long before 1960 forces began to grow and gather in a way that would create unprecedented pressures for Judeo-Christian tradition and the American culture. All three anchors would be attacked. Charles Darwin published, *The Origin of the Species By Means of Natural Selection or the Preservation of Favored Races in the Struggle for Life*, in 1859. It became known as the theory of evolution, purporting that all life forms evolved by chance over extremely long periods of time. Darwin's theory appeared to give scientific sanction to a concept that had been around for a very long time. Although it has been shown by Dr. Lloyd Stebbins and many others that evolution in its purist form is not possible, the theory of evolution became the basis for some to claim that God does not exist. *The first anchor, the Bible, came quickly under attack.* The theory of evolution has since become embedded throughout the nation's public school systems.

The relentless attack on the Bible was just the beginning. Since the emergence of the scientific method of investigation at the time of Sir Isaac Newton, there have been repeated attempts to apply it to every area of human endeavor, including the behavior of people. It was suggested that if all life formed by an evolutionary process, then other realms of civilizational development should also be amenable to long, slow evolutionary changes.

The Founders intended and declared the Constitution to be a firm anchor-like foundational document for the American culture. They knew that although societies change over time, the self-centered essence of human nature does not change. John Adams proclaimed, "We have no government armed with power capable of contending with human passions unbridled by morality and religion. Avarice, ambition, revenge, or gallantry, would break the strongest cords of our Constitution as a whale goes through a net. Our Constitution was made only for a moral and religious people. It is wholly inadequate to the government of any other."

If the "passions of men" were not voluntarily restrained and reigned-in by law and by Scripture, the Great American Experiment in self-government would fail. Yet, in modern times there has been a powerful movement claiming that the Constitution must be flexible and keep up with or evolve with the times. *Hence, the second anchor has been subjected to ruthless attack.*

Kinsey falsely claimed that the sexual and moral behavior of Americans was nowhere near the conservative beliefs that prevailed at the time. His personal mission was to destroy all the Biblical limits on sexual behavior. Morals had to evolve. His close friends in the legal profession were persuaded that the laws had to evolve to more closely match the supposed real behaviors of American society. Since then, thousands of laws prohibiting immoral behavior have been repealed.

Similarly, the family had to evolve (or devolve?) accordingly. The definition of "family" has been diluted to the point of near non-existence. A wave of no-fault divorce laws swept the country in the 1970s and 1980s, fracturing the concept of personal responsibility and guaranteeing record high divorce rates. The United States is among the few countries with the highest divorce rates in the world. *The third anchor has been unmercifully attacked.*

The stability of the family and sustainability of the American culture exist to the extent that we tenaciously hang on to all three anchors. Humanism attacks and undermines all three, setting adrift the ship of life, which will eventually be caught in the vortex of a perfect storm and sink. A culture without direction and purpose collapses. "Where *there is* no vision, the people perish." [*Proverbs 29:18 KJV*]

All three, once rock-solid, anchors have been continuously attacked for over 60 years. As before, where have the Judeo-Christian believers been? Ask any group of believers today to describe their beliefs. Typical responses will be "religious," "spiritual, but not religious," "somewhat religious," or "moderately religious." Alternatively, they may claim that their faith is "very important," "important," "moderately important," "somewhat important," or "relatively unimportant" to their daily lives. All such terms reflect some extent of compromise. What are they actually saying?

Many will intellectually agree that the Bible is the inspired, inerrant, Word of God, but it is merely an intellectual assent, not a spiritual conviction. Since the Bible is the ultimate anchor of the American culture and the other anchors, the founding documents and traditional family, are derived from the Bible, all three anchors are rock-solid because they are built on the foundation of God's perfect Word. Any deviation or erosion of that foundation must necessarily give man's imperfect thinking a priority higher than God. "Such "wisdom" does not come down from heaven but is earthly, unspiritual, demonic." [*James 3:15 NIV*] "For the wisdom of this world is foolishness in God's sight." [*1 Corinthians 3:19*

America: Dark Slide-Bright Future

NIV] "And he said to man, the fear of the Lord—that is wisdom; and to shun evil is understanding." [*Job 28;28 NIV*]

How can any honest believer replace any of God's perfect instructions for living with man's imperfect constructions? Abandoning God—to any extent—destroys the family, the Constitution, capitalism, and freedom. The result is a runaway government and tyranny. Now, more than ever before, believers MUST overlook their doctrinal differences and unite to save the family, the freedom that came from God, and the beloved American culture that has been blessed by God and the envy of the world for hundreds of years.

CHAPTER 6

THE TARGET IS YOUR FAMILY

Radical feminism is the most destructive and fanatical movement to come down to us from the Sixties. This is a revolutionary, not a reformist, movement, and it is meeting with considerable success. Totalitarian in spirit, it is deeply antagonistic to traditional Western culture and proposes the complete restructuring of society, morality, and human nature.

Judge Robert H. Bork[1]

Let marriage be held in honor among all...

Hebrews 18:4 NAS

BIG GUNS ARE AIMED AT YOUR FAMILY! WILL IT SURVIVE?

In modern America, God's grand and glorious institution, the family, is being ferociously attacked. The relentless and malicious attacks are aimed at the traditional family in general and *YOUR family in particular*.

Consider first the context of the modern American culture. Then wrestle with the grim and determined attacks by the *unprecedented number of highly organized groups determined to destroy YOUR family*. They have specific targets, a huge arsenal of devastating weapons, and massive power.

POWERFUL ANTI-FAMILY ENEMIES ALIGNED AGAINST YOUR FAMILY

- Evolutionists
- Radical feminists
- Multiculturalists
- Pornographers
- Planned Parenthood
- American Civil Liberties Union (ACLU)
- Liberal/Progressives
- LGBT Organizations
- Muslims/Islamists
- Abortion activists
- Socialists/Marxists
- Animal rights activists

<u>*All of these groups are Humanist or antagonistic to the American family or both*</u>. They have made man his own god. They are determined to reshape America in the socialist, Humanist mold, a "fundamental transformation."

Perhaps, like many, you have concluded that as a Judeo-Christian believer, "I don't belong to any of these groups nor do I support them." Therefore, they have nothing to do with me. **Wrong! Wrong! Dead wrong!** <u>*They have everything to do with YOU*</u>. <u>They ALL share a publically declared goal to destroy YOUR FAMILY</u>. They will mock your successes and cheer your failures. In the Internet Age of virtually no privacy and instant everything, you can no longer "fly under the radar" and be protected by a weekly trip to church or synagogue.

Collectively, the groups create a cultural climate that undermines and weakens the sanctity of life, the sanctity of marriage, and the sovereignty of the family. <u>*The statistically equivalent rates of abortion, divorce, and pornography use between conservative believers and atheists/agnostics unambiguously demonstrate that the body of believers has been severely and negatively compromised by the combined efforts of the anti-family groups*</u>.

TARGETS OF THE ANTI-FAMILY GROUPS INCLUDE YOUR FAMILY

To fundamentally transform America, the anti-family groups must have specific targets and objectives. A few of them are:

- <u>*Destroy the Biblical family INCLUDING YOURS*</u>
- Ridicule patriotism (an outgrowth of Judeo-Christian tradition)
- Substantially weaken the Unites States Constitution
- Undermine the concept of a representative republic (democracy)
- Abolish capitalism and the free enterprise system
- Denigrate the Founding Fathers
- Eliminate the sanctity marriage
- Destroy the sanctity of life
- Annihilate the sovereignty of the family

The God-created, God-ordained, Biblical family is the *only* real source of long-term cultural stability. A culture is stable only to the extent that the people consider the needs of others before the needs of self. It is an unassailable Biblical principle that can only be passed on to posterity through soulfully committed traditional families. The family is the heart and strength of the "Great American Experiment." *No nation has ever survived the breakdown of the family.*

The anti-family Humanist groups must destabilize, weaken, and eventually destroy the family to make the American culture receptive to massive change (fundamental transformation). The intent to deliberately destroy the institution of the family is well documented in their published writings.

Later discussions will identify the mind blowing weaponry and the sources of the massive power available to the anti-family groups.

Do not be discouraged. There will also be a challenge to protect YOUR FAMILY. Subsequent discussions will explain how.

STUNNING HEAVY ARTILLERY AMASSED BY THE ANTI-FAMILY GROUPS

Weapons are required to destroy the targets. The anti-family groups have assembled a formidable arsenal of <u>*powerful weapons aimed at YOUR family*</u>, including but not limited to.

- Political correctness, a means to shut down all opposing viewpoints, by eliminating freedom of speech.
- Unconditional abortion often paid for by the government
- Pornography use by children, women, and men
- No-fault divorce
- Social approval of cohabitation
- Encourage single-parent "families."
- Kinesian sex education
- Social approval of out-of-wedlock births
- Malignant welfare state establishing permanent dependence on government
- Effectively ban religion from public discourse by abusive interpretation of the First Amendment to the U.S. Constitution
- Legal recognition of same-sex "marriage"
- Theory of evolution
- Child adoption by same-sex couples
- Surrogate births for same-sex couples
- Unlimited government regulations of every area of life
- Easy student loans create dependence on government
- Promote massive change using the judicial system to bypass the voters
- Prioritize career over family, withdrawing women and love from the home

- Legal recognition of transgendered individuals.
- First promote "tolerance" of all manner of perverse behavior followed by legal recognition of "equality" of practitioners (*<u>establishes the moral equivalence of good and evil; lack of tolerance for sinful behavior is proclaimed "evil"</u>*)
- Government takeover of parental responsibilities
- Claimed racism
- Infanticide/euthanasia

FEARSOME POWER OF THE ANTI-FAMILY GROUPS

- The attackers have available the formidable and intimidating power of the:
- Highest level *politicians*
- Full weight of the *mainstream press*
- Highly publicized personal and moral failures of *sports and entertainment celebrities*
- Emotional and spiritual power of most of the *entertainment industry*
- Peer and cultural pressure of a *rapidly collapsing American culture*
- Corrupt *public school systems* that have become intellectually incompetent as well as emotionally and spiritually toxic
- Brute force of the *Federal government* facilitated by a runaway judiciary

Clearly, the big guns have become a prominent part of modern American culture. It is abundantly clear that one of their objectives is the destruction of the traditional Biblical American family. The many anti-family groups are powerful. They have identified specific targets, including you family, are armed with heavy artillery, and possess fearsome power. The situation may seem intimidating, but is no match for the power of God. "It is he who made the earth by his power, who established the world by his wisdom, and by his understanding stretched out the heavens." [*Jeremiah 10:12 ESV*] "The LORD your God is in your midst, a mighty one who will save; he will rejoice over you with gladness; he will quiet you by his love; he will exult over you with loud singing." [*Zephaniah 3:17 ESV*] "But Jesus looked at them and said, 'With man this is impossible, but with God all things are possible.'" [*Matthew 19:26 ESV*]

CHAPTER 6 NOTES

1. Robert H. Bork, *Slouching Towards Gomorrah: Modern Liberalism and American Decline*, (New York: Regan Books; HarperCollins Publishers. 1996) p. 194.

CHAPTER 7
FAMILY DEFENSE IS UP TO YOU

Government is not reason; it is not eloquence; it is force! Like fire, it is a dangerous servant and a fearful master.

George Washington

Hold on to the Constitution, for if the American Constitution should fail, there will be anarchy throughout the world.

Daniel Webster

Stand fast therefore in the liberty wherewith Christ hath made us free, and be not entangled again with the yoke of bondage.

Galatians 5:1 KJV

YOU MUST PROTECT YOUR FAMILY FROM CULTURAL DEVASTATION!

The Judeo-Christian family today faces a formidable array of big guns designed to weaken and destroy it. The family has already been directly substantially weakened by

1. Dilution (cohabitation)
2. Redefinition (any combination of people living together)
3. Government intrusion into every aspect of family life
4. Destruction of the sanctity of life
5. Decimation of the sanctity of marriage

6. Annihilation of the sovereignty of the family

The traditional family is virtually at war with the federal government. Many people would not choose a term as harsh as war. But the tension between the *sovereignty of the family* and the *sovereignty of the state* has undeniably escalated in recent decades.

GOVERNMENT INCREASINGLY BREACHES FAMILY SOVEREIGNTY

The family is the basic self-governing unit of all civilization. National or cultural cohesiveness and stability depend on the aggregation of cohesive families:

> Marriage makes a small state within the state. That bond breaks all other bonds; that law is found stronger than all later and lesser laws[1]...the small state founded on the sexes is at once the most voluntary and the most natural of all self-governing states.[2] *The Christian view of marriage conceives of the home as self-governing in a manner analogous to an independent state*[3]...In this way it is itself a sort of standing reformer of the State; for the State is judged by whether its arrangements bear helpfully or bear hardly on the human fullness and fertility of the free family.[4] *G.K. Chesterton*

By definition, a government controls (rules) or limits freedom of individuals and families for the common "good." Unless constitutionally limited, a government will grow without bounds, ultimately displacing the family, leading to tyranny. Consequently, there is a perpetual tension between the *sovereignty of the free family* and the *sovereignty of the controlling government*.

Families tend to break down as a result of a constellation of selfish decisions supported, facilitated, and encouraged by the government (divorce, abortion, pornography, euthanasia, infanticide, assisted suicide, career before family, allowing "strangers" to raise our children, uncontrolled personal debt, increasing dependence upon government and progressive dilution of the definition of what constitutes a family). While the clergy traditionally fights to preserve the family, the modern American government fights to destroy it.

Perpetual tension between the sovereign family and the sovereign government

PERPETUAL TENSION BETWEEN THE SOVEREIGN FAMILY AND THE SOVEREIGN GOVERNMENT

Families and individuals living in a Judeo-Christian culture seek to put others before self. Although doing so is a lifetime journey, the ongoing effort harmonizes many interpersonal relationships and much of society, even among those who are not adherents to Judeo-Christian tradition. When a culture such as the United States moves from a faith in God to a faith in evolution it migrates from an emphasis on serving others to serving self, producing sharp and dramatic increases in the most selfish decisions of all—those involving life and death.

Choices forbidden for millennia in Judeo-Christian and most other cultures first become legalized, and a short time later endorsed and even facilitated by active government promotion and financial support. The most selfish decisions ever made include divorce, abortion, euthanasia, allowing strangers to raise a married couple's children, and prematurely side-barring inconvenient relatives in institutions such as nursing homes. In a declining culture, those horrible, heart-wrenching decisions become the new norm. When Self reigns supreme, there is no limit to the evil that can be perpetrated by one person on another. At the national (cultural) level, the evil is readily cloaked in appealing language such as "pro-choice" or "death with dignity." No civilization has ever survived the breakdown of the family.

All governments (other than a constitutional republic purposefully designed to promote and reinforce the family) and radical movements (liberal-progressivism, socialism, fascism, communism, radical feminism, pornography, multiculturalism, and various "rights" movements, e.g. gay, lesbian, animal, etc.) seek the destruction of the traditional family as a means of creating chaos, which enables rapid migration to absolute governmental control.

> "Freedom is not a gift bestowed upon us by other men, but a right that belongs to us by the laws of God and nature. "
> *Ben Franklin*
> "God who gave us life gave us liberty. And can the liberties of a nation be thought secure when we have removed their only firm basis, a conviction in the minds of the people that these liberties are of the Gift of God?
> *Thomas Jefferson [Engraved on the walls of the Jefferson Memorial]*
> "Statesmen, my dear Sir, may plan and speculate for liberty, but it is Religion and Morality alone, which can establish the Principles upon which Freedom can securely stand.
> *John Adams*

The fight for freedom is a fight for:

- The sanctity of life
- The sanctity of marriage, and
- The sanctity and sovereignty of family

God created life; God created marriage; God created the family. Judeo-Christian culture and many other cultures have recognized the sanctity of life, marriage, and family for thousands of years. Any belief or action that compromises those anchors offends God and contributes to the eventual inescapable breakdown of a culture. There are no exceptions and no alternatives.

The god of science has produced the marvels of technology and many modern conveniences but has no influence on the human soul. Science cannot improve the internal well-being of a person but can and does contribute to the progressive isolation of individuals. Today, everyone seems to be almost continuously plugged into something. People are increasingly isolated in time and space cut off from a sense of the panorama of time reporting fewer close friends than ever before. The same isolation interferes with the growth of relationships among family members weakening and all too often causing the breakup of families. Further, the compromised beliefs and attitudes as well as painful emotions have a harsh and lasting negative ripple effect on other relatives, friends, neighbors, and business associates.

> **The state breaches family sovereignty by:**
> - Encouraging divorce, abortion, euthanasia, assisted suicide
> - Removing children from their family
>   - Tacitly for ever increasing amounts of "education"
>   - Physically for an ever-widening list of alleged "abuses"
> - Dilution/diffusion (ever broadening definition of "family" to include a growing list of "alternative lifestyles")
> - Increasing control over personal health, including life and death decisions
> - Promoting pornography, radical feminism and materialism, which undermine and scatter the family
> - Attacking traditional roles of family members
> - Facilitating a progressively increasing dependence on government
> - Replacing traditional family values with evolution-rooted postmodern views (no god; no absolute/objective truth; no single set of universal values)
> - Promoting multiculturalism over traditional Judeo-Christian culture and values
> - Adopting a suffocating array of ever increasing over-regulations

For example, when parents divorce or choose abortion they almost assure that surviving children and grandchildren will perhaps years later make similar decisions. The same self-serving decisions substantially increase the likelihood that grown siblings and other relatives and friends will follow the same path. The decisions that used to be shocking become more acceptable among people who personally know others who have made such decisions and have appeared to have moved on in a positive way.

But outward appearances often provide an attractive veneer covering inward anxiety and pain. The government's relentless attacks on marriage and family and active and professional promotion of abortion readily facilitate ungodly decisions. In some cases the government can sponsor the veneer but can do nothing to improve the condition of the soul.

Why is it that most people go to the churches and synagogues to get married, a relatively simple procedure, but go to the government to be supposedly released from the vows they made to God and the covenant they made with each other? Many billions of tax dollars are required to support the divorce and abortion industries. Today, the "we the people" are expected to pay for the failures of others. Where did the government get the authority to overrule or dissolve vows made

> "Those who expect to reap the blessings of freedom must, like men, undergo the fatigue of supporting it."
> *Thomas Paine*
> "There are more instances of the abridgement of the freedom of the people by the gradual and silent encroachment of those in power, than by violent and sudden usurpation."
> *James Madison*

to God? Answer: The government merely assumed the authority as the product of evolution-rooted thinking. The traditional family is virtually at war with the federal government. Many people would not choose a term as harsh as war. But the tension between the sovereignty of the family and the sovereignty of the state has undeniably escalated in recent decades.

Today, there is little push back from Christians and Jews, because they have become spiritually anesthetized by the lure of materialism, the magnet of technology, and at least tacit if not full acceptance of the theory of evolution, as well as at least tacit acceptance of radical feminist, pornography, and multiculturalist bunker busters and similar social movements as well as the overwhelming peer pressure of political correctness.

There is some push back by home schooling families who band to together to pool resources and create social interaction opportunities for the children. Some families are reluctantly drawn into legal disputes with the government that challenge the propriety and processes of home schooling. Most Christians are represented only by national groups such as Focus on the Family, (Insert Image_12 to the left of text)the American Family Association and nationally known Christian law firms that routinely intervene in cases where a plaintiff seeks to obstruct or prohibit God-given liberties. Many such legal cases involve interpretations of the separation of church and state or the removal of Christian symbols from public view. Note that the plaintiff is nearly always an atheist activist. A plaintiff of another religious faith is rare. The federal government's endgame is a neutralized symbolic state approved church cited for propaganda purposes. The rest of the body of Christ is eventually forced underground. Sound like Russia? China? Of course. Could it happen here? You bet it could! Despite the awesome work of the well-known Christian organizations, their efforts are limited — constrained by an indifferent body of believers.

The preceding chapters considered the fall of the United States from a cohesive sustainable Judeo-Christian culture to the current fragmented unstable one that is not sustainable. The rate of the fall has accelerated in recent decades. It is rooted in a scientifically weak, but politically strong theory of evolution enable by an ever narrowing and restrictive definition of science. Although the fall has become the greatest crises in United States history, the remedy is awesome.

CHAPTER 7 NOTES

1. G.K. Chesterton, *Collected Works, Volume IV: What's Wrong with the World; The Superstition of Divorce; Eugenics and Other Evils*, (San Francisco: Ignatius Press, 1987), p. 270.
2. Ibid. p. 237.
3. Ibid. p. 421.
4. G.K. Chesterton, *Collected Works, Volume IV: What's Wrong with the World; The Superstition of Divorce; Eugenics and Other Evils*, (San Francisco: Ignatius Press, 1987) p. 422.

CHAPTER 8

GOD'S POWER IS THE GREATEST

Faith is the central problem of this age. [It is a choice] between irreconcilable opposites—God or Man, Soul or Mind, Freedom or Communism.

Whittaker Chambers[1]

The fool hath said in his heart, there is no God.

Psalms 14:1 KJV

GOD'S POWER AND LOVE ARE FAR STRONGER AND LONGER LASTING THAN ANY OTHER

At the beginning of the classic movie, *The Ten Commandments*, director Cecil B. DeMille did something remarkable. He walked out on a stage to preface the movie with a few heartfelt comments:

> Ladies and Gentlemen; young and old; this may seem an unusual procedure, speaking to you before the picture begins, but we have an unusual subject: the story of the birth of freedom; the story of Moses...The theme of this picture is whether men ought to be ruled by God's laws or whether they are to be ruled by the whims of a dictator like Rameses. Are men the property of the State or are they free souls under God? This same battle continues throughout the world today. *Our intention was not to create a story, but to*

be worthy of the divinely inspired story created 3,000 years ago in the five books of Moses.[2]

DeMille's understanding of the importance of God's laws was further clarified in the souvenir book distributed along with the movie:

> The Ten Commandments are not rules to obey as a personal favor to God. They are fundamental principles without which mankind cannot live together—THE TEN COMMANDMENTS are not laws. They are THE LAW. Man has made 32,000,000 laws since they were handed down to Moses on Mount Sinai more than three thousand years ago, but he has never improved on God's law.[3]

The movie was clearly DeMille's labor of love. It dramatizes a Biblical story that was a favorite of the American founders. The story of the Exodus was such a powerful influence on the founders that an early draft of the Great Seal of the United States recommended by Thomas Jefferson, John Adams, and Ben Franklin portrayed an image of the freed Israelites led by God's pillar of fire.[4]

Clearly, the greatest and most complete source of information about God is the Bible. Most conservative believers would readily agree that it is the inspired inerrant Word of God.

But what happened? Have we become spiritually numbed by the uniquely American luxury of having a shelf full of Bibles and a weekly dose of sugar-coated sermons? The rampant compromises among believers scream a resounding, "Yes!" Wow! Chew on that one for a while. Perhaps, for many, the notion that the Bible is the inspired Word of God is merely intellectual assent, rather than a soul-deep conviction.

A military analogy is helpful. Anyone who has ever been in the military knows that with rare exceptions, disobeying an order is unthinkable. Obedience is deeply embedded in the military culture, because in combat there is no time to appoint a committee to study the situation. The assumption is that the highest ranking onsite officer has the greatest training and experience and therefore has the greatest probability of making the most effective decisions at the lowest casualty rate.

Similarly, we are soldiers in the spiritual battle between good and evil, facing the arsenal of big guns aimed at our families. The battle between the advocates of the Judeo-Christian worldview and the advocates of the evolution-driven humanistic worldview has been astonishingly aggressive. The extreme intensity and relentless endurance of the battle strongly suggests the involvement of an unseen power or powers. That world of unseen powers we call the spirit world. God defines good and evil in Scripture. His love fuels and drives, or should drive the lives of believers. Pride leveraged by Satan drives the lives of advocates of Humanism. In his book, *Angels*, Billy Graham explained:

> We live in a perpetual battlefield...The wars among the nations on earth are mere popgun affairs compared to the fierceness of battle in the spiritual unseen world. This invisible spiritual conflict is waged around us incessantly and unremittingly. Where the Lord works, Satan's forces hinder; where angel beings carry out divine directives, the devils rage. All this comes about because the powers of darkness press their counterattack to recapture the ground held for the glory of God...
>
> Since the fall of Lucifer, that angel of light and son of the morning, there has been no respite in the bitter Battle of the Ages. Night and day Lucifer, the master craftsman of the devices of darkness, labors to thwart God's plan of the ages. We can find inscribed on every page of human history the

consequences of the evil brought to fruition by the powers of darkness with the devil in charge. Satan never yields an inch, nor does he ever pause in his opposition to the plan of God to redeem the "cosmos" from his control.[5]

Our orders are issued by the Commanding General of the Universe. His orders are always perfect and guarantee success. They are found in the Bible.

God's orders are often expressed as commands. If the word command is not used, the orders are nearly always written in the active voice or as an imperative. <u>The essence of a command is that it is 1) non-negotiable, 2) not optional, 3) do it now, and 4) no excuses</u>. Of course, His love for us is so great that He gives us the awesome gift of free will that allows us to choose to be disobedient. Nevertheless, God's Word is directive, because He knows that the natural penalty or consequence for disobedience is painful, often rippling through many others.

Obedience to God is always much more beneficial for us than disobedience. The gap between God's wisdom and ours is so vast that obedience should be an inescapably obvious no-brainer. But it is a lesson we need to constantly relearn, because of the relentless interference of pride.

*The Bible is **not** simply a guidebook.* Suggestions or flexible guidelines are rare. Long ago at the beginning of an engineering career, my Dad offered an important piece of advice. He said, "The boss never makes a suggestion; it may sound like a suggestion, but it's not a suggestion." Dad was urging me to treat my boss's apparent suggestions as an order or direct instruction. The advice has held up well throughout my career. If it is important to treat the suggestions of an earthly boss as an order, how much more important is it to treat any of God's apparent Biblical suggestions or guidelines as an order or commandment?

God gave us the Bible to be revered. It is our most treasured and sacred possession. If the house is on fire and you are fleeing, you cannot carry very much, but at least grab the Bible. "*All* scripture *is* given by inspiration of God, and *is* profitable for doctrine, for reproof, for correction, for instruction in righteousness: That the man of God may be perfect, thoroughly furnished unto all good works." [*2 Timothy 3: 16-17 KJV*]

When you have soulfully restored the Bible to life's highest priority and most treasured of all possessions, your family can survive relentless attack by the powerful and well-organized anti-family enemies. Here are the Judeo-Christian weapons.

- God's power
- God's infinite love
- Prayer (God's direct personal communications line)
- Bible (God's specific directions—not guidelines—for life)

<u>The family must be viewed as Dad, Mom, and the children against the universe. Marriage is permanent; abortion is never an option; family and children are the highest priority in this life. No exceptions</u>!

The wholeness and sanctity of marriage, family, and life at all stages must be unconquerable by government as God designed it and as the Founders codified it. Abraham Kuyper and G. K. Chesterton both called it the *sovereignty of the family*. It is in constant tension with the *sovereignty of the state*. <u>*If believers are unwilling to defend God's turf, the government will take it away*</u>. "...Render to Caesar the things that are Caesar's, and to God the things that are God's." [*Mark 12:17 KJV*] Every believer must deeply and irrevocably commit to never giving unto government that which is God's.

GOD IS THE GREATEST DEFENSE AND THE GREATEST OFFENSE

The current situation nationally and individually is overwhelmingly urgent. The crisis is undeniable. It is now up to YOU to save America and the family. Here is the plan. *Here is what must happen and happen quickly.*

All believers' attitudes and commitments

- *Pray*—Thus far little has been said about prayer. It has been assumed that most Jews and Christians already know and understand the power and importance of regular communication with God through prayer. Cultural change is massive; YOUR PRAYERS are a critical and essential foundation for any such change. Unless there is Divine support, the results of our combined efforts will be limited and have little cultural impact.
- *Cultivate holistic thinking*—Understand and identify with God's holistic views of life and the universe. Understanding the whole, far-reaching, long-term impacts of individual decisions turns currently apparently controversial life choices into no-brainers in favor of the Biblical standard.
- *Develop a soul-deep conviction that God's commands are an expression of His love*—Most of God's scriptural directions are expressed as non-optional commands as an expression of His love, not because He is the dictatorial general of the universe. He knows that virtually every time we insist on doing something our way, rather than His way, there is an inevitable unpleasant price—sometimes a very high price—to pay.
- *Soulfully commit to active lifestyle character development*—Many believers in the modern American culture have lost a sense of mission. That mission, which you must accept by

Scriptural command, is to grow in character moving continuously toward greater godly character so that ultimately the "wisdom of age" has real practical meaning once again, as it has for many millennia. Wisdom must be pursued on a conscious continuous basis to counter the relentless cultural pounding that pushes believers toward ungodly, unwise compromise. Wisdom grows to the extent we choose to serve others.

- *Become real full-time, not just Sabbath morning, conduits for God's love* — Ultimate love is God's love, which is characterized by ultimate giving — giving of Himself for us. God's love is spiritual energy fueling our love as it applies to all interpersonal relationships, which can only grow to the extent of our giving. It is not anywhere near sufficient to pray, preach, and sing about God's love on Sabbath mornings and then "raise hell" the rest of the week, a pattern far too common in modern America. YOU must become a full time conduit of God's love. It is the natural result of habitually loving others before self, a habit that must be consciously cultivated. A habit is a mental "muscle." Unless it is continually exercised, it will atrophy.

- *Continuously demonstrate virtuous living in all areas at all times, regardless of the cost* — Deliberately and routinely make choices designed to build character and wisdom. In our culture, it is a habit that must be deliberately cultivated or it is unlikely to happen at all.

- *Commit to being an uncompromisingly positive role model* — YOU are a role model; the only choice available is to be a positive or negative role model. In a mere four generations, YOU will directly or indirectly influence nearly 2,000,000 people, from direct descendants to virtually everyone with whom you and your descendants come in contact. Consequently, it is inescapably important that you routinely choose to be a positive role model in all decisions large and small.

Family attitudes and commitments

- *Recapture a real lifelong uncompromising commitment to marriage*—The scriptural God-defined and established concept of marriage is the only arrangement that can firmly establish the cohesiveness of the family and the sustainability of the national culture. The progressive dilution of the family concept inevitably leads to chaos and eventually to a government in total control of every aspect of life. The path is strewn with rapidly escalating pain and suffering and freedom is lost.
- An ironclad commitment to Biblical marriage is the role model intended for children to experience through both natural parents. It ultimately produces the greatest satisfaction in life for parents and their descendants as well as the greatest continuity and cultural sustainability across many generations. Since neither spouse can be completely joyful while the other is discouraged, the commitment to lifelong marriage has a built-in incentive to love the spouse before self. As the Nike commercial says, "Just do it!" You'll be glad you did even if it seems painful for a while—perhaps quite a while in some cases.
- *Recapture the priority and ultimate responsibility of families and child rearing*—Children cannot be raised by strangers with the expectation of building and embedding soul-deep spiritual values in their soul. No one but a child's parents can provide the powerful role models required to establish the foundation of values and biblical priorities that will enable a child to eventually make the right biblical large and small life choices, producing a life portrait that will be admired by others, satisfying to self, and

rewarded by God. Remember that nearly 2,000,000 people are ultimately depending on YOU to make the right choices. Another 2,000,000 people are depending on each of your descendants to make the right life choices. The highest priority choices begin with the children that you bring into this world, intentionally or otherwise.

- *Recapture the parental responsibility for the education of their children* — By God's command, the Old Testament assigns the primary responsibility for educating the children to the parents. The assignment has never changed. That responsibility can be augmented by the churches and synagogues as well as faith-based schools. Throughout most of United States history the public schools extended the same parental responsibility. But evolution-rooted humanism has elevated man to becoming his own god and reduced the public educational system to educating the intellect alone and indoctrinating children with the principles and precepts of humanism, while specifically and forcefully excluding any references to God or Biblical principles. Parents had enormous influence on the schools until recent decades. Today, parents are virtually denied any real educational influence as progressively more decisions are made in Washington, D.C. Parents must urgently and absolutely recapture the responsibility for educating their children.

Church and synagogue attitudes and commitments

- *Restructure churches to actually support the family, rather than dispersing the family* — Churches and synagogues tend to create an array of age, gender, and marital status-based programs and activities that effectively segregate and contribute to the weakening and eventual breakdown of families. The faith-based organizations must reorganize to support families by physically bringing them together for routine weekly family activities. An annual family picnic does not even come close to satisfying the need.

- *Emphasize serving God by serving one person at a time*—Serving the needs of one specific person at a time breaks the cultural stranglehold of excessive materialism. Service is not an accumulation of busyness at faith-based institutions. Real spiritual growth-producing service is meeting the needs of real people, one person at a time. Individual service produces spiritual growth in humility, forgiveness, mercy, long suffering, and a servant's spirit in both the server and the one served.

The duality of spiritual growth is illustrated in Shakespeare's, *The Merchant of Venice*. In Portia's famous courtroom speech, she argues in part, "The quality of mercy is not strain'd…it is twice bless'd; it blesseth him that gives and him that takes…it becomes the throned monarch better than his crown…it is an attribute to God himself; and earthly power doth then show likest God's when mercy seasons justice."[6] We have become far too dependent upon the clergy and an endless array of "programs" to meet the needs of carefully identified groups of people. Although the needs of many in the groups may be met, the overdependence bypasses the awesome spiritual and character growth of the server that occurs when an individual server directly meets the needs of the one served on a person- to-person basis.

- *Build a large number of faith-based schools as expeditiously as possible*—Despite the efforts of many sincere people, the public schools are in a shambles and many faith-based schools are equipped primarily to serve rather wealthy families. The only real remedy is for churches and synagogues to use existing buildings to establish large numbers of affordable faith-based schools. Unless Judeo-Christian believers recapture the education of their children, through the churches and synagogues, the American culture will continue its unrestrained march to humanistic chaos and total government domination.

The modern American government Goliath is fearsome to behold. But YOU have available far more than young David's five smooth stones. God Himself and His infinite love are far greater than all the cultural and physical weapons ever devised.

CHAPTER 8 NOTES

1. Whittaker Chambers, *Witness*, (Washington: Regnery Gateway, 1980).
2. The American Vision, retrieved from http://americanvision.org/7804/the-ten-commandments-moral-anarchy-and-the-secular-state/#sthash.i2jIjdFc.dpbs, View on http://www.youtube.com/watch?v=o8iNvzzak5U
3. Ibid.
4. W. Cleon Skousen, *The 5000 Year Leap: A Miracle That Changed the World*, (National Center for Constitutional Studies. 2006) 17-18.
5. Billy Graham, *Angels: God's Secret Agents*, (Garden City, New York: Doubleday & Company, 1975) 66-68.
6. William Shakespeare [Introduction, and notes explanatory and critical, by Rev. Henry N. Hudson, LL.D.], *Merchant of Venice*. (Boston, Ginn & Company, Publishers, 1903) 169

CHAPTER 9

THE GOD-DESIGNED FAMILY IS IMPREGNABLE

There is nothing in any other social relations in any way parallel to the mutual attraction of the sexes. By missing this simple point, the modern world has fallen into a hundred follies...There is no dispute about the purpose of Nature in creating such an attraction. It would be more intelligent to call it the purpose of God; for Nature can have no purpose unless God is behind it.

G. K. Chesterton

The happy State of Matrimony is, undoubtedly, the surest and most lasting Foundation of Comfort and Love; the Source of all that endearing Tenderness and Affection which arises from Relation and Affinity; the grand Point of Property; the Cause of all good Order in the World, and what alone preserves it from the utmost Confusion; and, to sum up all, the Appointment of infinite Wisdom for these great and good Purposes [sic].

Benjamin Franklin

Lo, children are an heritage of the Lord and the fruit of the womb is his reward...Happy is the man that hath his quiver full of them.

Psalms 127:3-5 KJV

SURVIVAL SKILLS FOR YOUR FAMILY

The forces aligned against the family are determined to weaken the family by dilution, redefinition, and government encroachment. They intend to destroy the sanctity of life, the sanctity of marriage, and the sovereignty of the family. However, there is hope. You have available an astonishing defense as well as incredibly powerful offensive weapons.

Mere intellectual agreement with the list of Judeo-Christian weapons is of little value. They are only useable to the extent of your soul-deep, uncompromising, irrevocable commitment to:

- Live a fully God-directed life in every area, all day, every day
- Visibly become the salt of the earth
- Visibly be the light of the world
- Actively be an ambassador for the Messiah, by living as an unassailable role model.

<u>Uncompromising conviction will suppress the barrier of pride and open the conduit of your life, for God's love to flow through. His infinite love will be manifested through YOU as **humility, forgiveness, mercifulness, longsuffering, and a servant's spirit**</u>. These are the visible components of love.

To the extent that others see godly character in us, they will become envious. "I say then, Have they stumbled that they should fall? God forbid: but *rather* through their fall salvation *is come* unto the Gentiles, for <u>to provoke them to jealousy</u>." [*Romans 11:11 KJV*]

We become visible and an active positive role model as we grow in godly character. People see godly character as increased confidence, resilience in the face of daily stresses, and an inner joy that is unshakable. It is an image that is real. It provokes the jealousy described in Romans. The jealousy inspires questions about your strength of character, triggering natural and amazingly comfortable opportunities to share your faith. Now, consider the genius of God's family.

THE GENIUS OF GOD'S FAMILY

The traditional family is one of the most awesome, breathtaking, and vitally important of all of God's magnificent creations! God's multidimensional portrait of the family is so eloquent and astonishingly beautiful that it makes Leonardo da Vinci's Mona Lisa look like a cartoon character. The extraordinarily beautiful partnership between the husband and wife springs from the holistic and pervasive appreciation of God. Here's why:

- God's portrait stabilizes and provides coherence to the family.
- The stabilized family builds stability and coherence into the national culture.
- A stable culture assures continuity of values across future generations.
- God's portrait facilitates growth of the God-ordained marriage partnership and family.
- Married people are happier.
- Married people are healthier.
- Family is life's boot camp for children, instilling virtues and guiding growth.
- True family-centered families—as opposed to career-centered family arrangements reduce crime.
- True family-centered families—as opposed to career-centered family arrangements reduce drug abuse.
- A loving family experience facilitates interpersonal relationships outside the family, enhancing the richness of career, hobby, volunteer, and recreational experiences.

- God's portrait enables family members to practice humility, forgiveness, mercy, longsuffering, and a servant's spirit in a loving, nonthreatening environment.
- The positive character embedded in family members—parents and children—is carried to the outside community throughout life. Children grow to the extent that parents are good role models and teachers; parents grow as they lovingly and consistently deal with childhood rebellion.
- Family members learn to overcome pride by serving other family members.
- The family is an incubator for building God-ordained intellectual, emotional, and spiritual views and values (character development).
- The family aligned with God's portrait ultimately leaves the greatest of all possible legacies.
- The family aligned with God's portrait is the married couple's gift back to God.
- The family aligned with God's portrait inspires frequent, comfortable, and nonthreatening opportunities for faith sharing.

Each family member is an ambassador of the family and family culture, which is a reflection of God's presence or His absence. It is the parents' responsibility to grow themselves from the character of natural sin-scarred man to the character of God, training their children to grow with them. *The parents must be what they want their children to become*. If so, the children will also grow in godly character and eventually pass on the godly legacy. Family is the 1) boot camp for life, 2) the training ground for building and developing character (parents and children), and 3) The God-created, God-ordained basic unit of civilization. Passing on godly character to children and as many other people as possible is life's most important responsibility.

This life is a relay not a sprint. We accept the family and cultural baton from the last generation; guard it, protect it, and improve upon it; and then pass the baton on to the next generation. Godly growth and character are cultivated only by serving the needs of others (no shortcuts). "…the son of Man did not come to be served, but to serve, and to give his life as a ransom for many." [*Matthew 20:28 & Mark 10:45 NIV*]

The husband is responsible for material well-being and spiritual leadership, but the wife is responsible for emotional well-being and spiritual well-being as well as the distribution and use of the material gain. If a husband must work in a dirty corrupted world, his wife must make the home a spiritual shower.

The woman is the anchor (stability) and the heart (life of the home). Her responsibility is to make the home the most desirable place in the universe. The man's job is to make hers easy by providing material resources, emotional support, and loving spiritual leadership. When the woman leaves the home for fulltime employment, the life goes out of the home like the air out of a punctured balloon or a flat tire. The home that was once full of love becomes merely a house filled only with furniture, a place where family members only come home to sleep. To be the anchor and heart of the home, the woman must be part of a mutual ironclad, irrevocable, "'til death do us part" marriage. *"What therefore God hath joined together, let not man put asunder"* (non-optional). [*Matthew 19:6; Mark 10:9 KJV*] The kids want to come home, because Mom's there; Dad wants to come home, because his family is there. Together, Dad and Mom are superheroes.

DAD AND MOM ARE SUPERHEROES

Both the Old and New Testaments of the Bible summarize the Ten Commandments into just two. "'Love the Lord your God with all your heart and with all your soul and with all your mind.' This is the first and greatest commandment. And the second is like it: 'Love your neighbor as yourself.' All the Law and the Prophets hang on these two commandments." [*Matthew 22:37-40; Deuteronomy 6:5; Leviticus 19:18 NIV*] Both commandments represent ultimate love characterized by extreme giving. The first is a vertical love of God; the second is a horizontal love of others.

Consider how those two commandments uniquely apply to marriage. Scripture explains the marriage relationship:

<u>Submitting yourselves one to another in the fear (reverence, awe) of God</u>. Wives, submit yourselves unto your own husbands, as unto the Lord. For the husband is the head of the wife, even as Christ is the head of the church: and he is the savior of the body. Therefore as the church is subject unto Christ, so let the wives be to their own husbands in everything. Husbands, love your wives, even as Christ also loved the church, and gave himself for it; that he might sanctify and cleanse it with the washing of water by the word, that he might present it to himself a glorious church, not having spot, or wrinkle, or any such thing; but that it should be holy and without blemish. [*Ephesians 5:21-28 KJV (emphasis added)*]

A husband must give himself for his family so they may become as perfect and blameless as is humanly possible. *<u>The husband and wife are mutual givers</u>*, but there is more, much more.

The earthly marriage is a representation of an eternal relationship with God. The Lord is illustrated scripturally as the bridegroom coming for his bride, the worldwide body of believers. "Let us rejoice and be glad and give him (Messiah) glory! For the wedding of the Lamb (Yeshua; Jesus) has come, and his bride has made herself ready...blessed are those who are invited to the wedding supper of the Lamb...These are the true words of God." [*Revelation 19:7&9 NIV*] The Bible further clarifies that the apostle John, "saw the holy city, new Jerusalem, coming down from God out of heaven prepared as a bride adorned for her husband." [*Revelation 21:2 KJV*]

Scripturally, the order of the universe is that the Lord is the bridegroom and the body of believers is the bride. Of course, in any earthly marriage the man is the bridegroom and the bride is the beautiful woman spectacularly dressed in a white wedding gown walking down the aisle to meet her man. But in a larger sense, the bride is not just the woman at the ceremony, the bride is the woman and by extension the children she later produces, often referred to as the fruit of her womb. The husband is required to love the wholeness of his bride, i.e. the wholeness of his family, even as the Messiah also loved the church, to the point of the husband's own death if necessary.

Fallows magnificently explains, "The husband is the 'house band,' the earthly giver of life, uniting the divine with the human in the supreme function of fatherhood." The wife is 'the weaver,' shaping and coloring in the prenatal and postnatal influences of sacred motherhood the destinies of her offspring."[1] "As the "earthly giver of life, uniting the divine with the human," the husband/father becomes the role model for "the first and greatest commandment" to "Love the Lord your God with all your heart and with all your soul and with all your mind."

As the "weaver," the wife/mother is the connection between the past and future generations of her family, but also the past and future generations of the culture. She is the role model for the second summary commandment to 'Love your neighbor as yourself.' Shannon clarifies,

Mothers constitute the only universal agent of civilization. Nature has placed in her hands both infancy and youth. The vital interest of America hang largely upon the influence of mothers."[2] The queen that sits upon the throne of home, crowned and sceptered as none other ever can be, is—mother. Her enthronement is complete, her reign unrivaled, and the moral issues of her empire are eternal. "Her children rise up, and call her blessed." Rebellious at times, as the subjects of her government may be, she rules them with marvelous patience, winning tenderness and undying love. She so presents and exemplifies divine truth, that it reproduces itself in the happiest development of childhood—character and life...An ounce of mother is worth more than a pound of clergy.[3]

Sadly, far too many dads in modern America fail to carry out their God-assigned, high- priority, family responsibilities, either due to a lack of holistic understanding, pornography, or the powerful lure of excessive materialism. Far too many moms fall short by not being there and available for raising the children. Together, such parents effectively sacrifice their children on the altar of the false gods of materialism, pornography, or other selfish pursuits. However, *when Dad and Mom lovingly and enthusiastically become God's family, the results can be deeply heartwarming and sometimes even breathtaking. When they do not, the results can range from troublesome to tragic*.

Some time ago, I devoted seven years to meeting virtually all the needs and providing around-the-clock care for my terminally ill late wife. She endured a neurodegenerative condition similar to Alzheimer's disease. After her passing, a well-wisher said. "You really sacrificed a lot during those years." I thanked her and replied that it did not seem like I sacrificed anything. Providing total care for her was more important than anything else I could have been doing during that time. It was a monumentally life-changing experience, a soul-deep lesson in selfless love. The experience has had long-term impacts on me and those around me and will continue to do so far into the future.

Together, fueled by God's infinite supply of love, Dad and Mom become virtual superheroes, an incredibly awesome team stabilizing God's brilliantly designed family and the national culture as a whole. A child forms a vertical relationship with God, primarily, though not exclusively, through the role model of the father; a child forms horizontal relationships with others within and beyond the family primarily, though not exclusively, through the role model of the mother. The complementary combination produces godly character in the child. The actions of role modeling build character in the parents. The character of every family member extends outward to the community and the nation.

That is God's grand design for Dad and Mom. What incredible superheroes!

GOD'S AWESOME LOVING FAMILY

The genius of the traditional family created by God, and supported by virtually every civilization throughout the 6,000 years of recorded history, rests on a foundation of an irrevocable, complementary and wholly pervasive partnership between a man and a woman (marriage), which is unique and impregnable. "...a man [shall] leave father and mother and shall cleave to his wife; and they twain shall be one flesh..." [*Matthew 19:5-6 KJV*] "What therefore God hath joined together, let not man put asunder." (non-optional) [*Matthew 19:6; Mark 10:9 Romans 12:2*] "...let each esteem other better than themselves." [*Philippians 2:3 KJV*] Pride goeth before destruction and a haughty spirit before a fall." [*Proverbs 16:18 KJV*] "Self-love [pride] ... is the sole antagonist of virtue, leading us constantly by our propensities to self-gratification in violation of our moral duties to others." *Thomas Jefferson*

The headship of the husband functions only to the extent of his wife's support even when he makes a wrong decision, e.g. ill-advised investment, for which the entire family may suffer the financial, emotional, and spiritual consequences. The shared sacrifice strengthens the family. Similarly, only a foolish husband would summarily ignore his wife's earnest counsel.

The cohesiveness of the marriage increases as the man and woman continually defer to each other through routine expressions of humility, forgiveness, mercy, longsuffering, and a servant's spirit. Pride is regularly sacrificed as each grows in the character of God. <u>*Collectively, the love and solidarity of the parents is a model for building character in the children. Character is more caught than taught*</u>.

Although the parents exhibit the same deferential character with respect to the children, the parents also establish firm physical/temporal boundaries aligned with God's moral boundaries. The parental boundaries are a visible expression of their love of the children. Since the mother typically has more time with the children, she is the primary character builder supported by the strength and stability of her "'til-death-do-us-part" committed husband. The parents support each other's decisions even when there is disagreement. <u>*The parent's ongoing expressions of love are the child's "security blanket."*</u>

"And beside this, giving all diligence, add to your faith virtue; and to virtue knowledge; and to knowledge temperance; and to temperance patience; and to patience godliness; and to godliness brotherly kindness; and to brotherly kindness charity...he that lacketh these things is blind, and cannot see afar off..." [*II Peter 1:5-7 & 9 KJV*]

A cohesive stable marriage produces a cohesive stable family, which becomes a cohesive stable national culture assuring stability and continuity throughout many generations of time. <u>**No culture has ever survived the breakdown of the family**</u>.

THE MIRACLE OF GOD'S FAMILY CHILD

When a child is conceived, he/she is endowed by the Creator with a new eternal soul; after an earthly life, the individual's soul is transported to Heaven, if God's saving grace has been accepted or is eternally lost to Hell, if God has been rejected. **_A mother's highest calling is to introduce that soul (child) to the universe_**.

The child—often called a miracle of God—arrives knowing nothing except what he/she is taught by the parents, primarily the mother. The child's lifetime ability to enjoy the fullness of the human experience is largely dependent on that maternal introduction, during childhood. _When the mother is substantially absent, the child has little opportunity to soulfully learn the anchor-like virtues which would otherwise establish a lifelong pattern of godly decisions_. Of course there are uncontrollable circumstances such as a death in the family or an unwanted divorce the create single-parent situations. Despite the obvious challenges of the situation the godly single parent may be shrouded in God's protective grace.

Putting a child in a day care center is a bit like putting a dog in a kennel; both are for selfish reasons. If you react negatively to that statement, perhaps reading on will soften the blow. Note that a home schooler can learn in an hour or so as much as another child can learn in a whole day at public school. Imagine the impact of a full-time mother!

Further, the parent's influence, especially that of the mother, extends through the generations of grandchildren, great-grandchildren, and great-great-grandchildren. Consider the positive and negative impacts of Dad and Mom's influence. "But from everlasting to everlasting the Lord's love is with those who fear him and his righteousness with their children's children with those who keep his covenant and remember to obey his precepts [_Psalms 103:17 NIV_]"and "...he punishes the children and their children for the sins of the fathers to the third and fourth generation [*Exodus 34:7b NIV*]."

In addition, the richness of the life experience is dependent on establishing a continuing pattern of godly choices. "Be careful to obey all these regulations I am giving you, so that it may always go well with you and your children after you, because you will be *doing what is good and right in the eyes of the Lord your God* [*Deuteronomy 12:28 NIV*]."

Consider that the mother's children, grandchildren, great-grandchildren, and great-great-grandchildren influence the lives of thousands of others, preferably in a positive godly way. What an awesome sacred responsibility God has assigned to the mother!

"...the only people who either can or will give individual care, to each of the individual children, are their individual parents[4] (*G.K. Chesterton*)." Why is it that a woman will slave for a stranger (boss), but object to serving her husband with whom she voluntarily chose to bind herself for life?[5] Of course, God requires ultimate sacrificial love by the husband. (*Ephesians 5:25*)."

GOD ASSIGNED TO THE PARENTS PRIMARY RESPONSIBILITY FOR CHILDREN'S EDUCATION

Scripture assigns to parents the primary responsibility of educating their children. That assignment directly from God has never changed. In time, the parents were aided by religious institutions assuring a seamless character building process from birth to adulthood and beyond. Eventually, government schools assumed the responsibility for educating the children.

Initially, the government sponsored public schools supported the spiritual mission so well that the parents and religious institutions began to abandon much of their God-assigned responsibilities for educating the children. But, beginning in the 1960s, the government kicked God out of the schools eventually banning most forms of religious expression in schools and virtually all other public places.

Consequently, today's public educational system is experiencing a major crisis. It has been hijacked by the liberal progressive movement and deprived of emotional and spiritual influences in order to emphasize the "academics," in preparation for the assumed priority of career over family in the life of every rising young man and young woman. Evolution-driven materialism recognizes no other educational goals.

In contrast, Martin Luther proclaimed, "I would advise no one to send his child where the Holy Scriptures are not supreme. Every institution that does not unceasingly pursue the study of God's Word becomes corrupt…I greatly fear that the [schools], unless they teach the Holy Scriptures diligently and impress them on the young students, are wide gates to Hell." Take control of education as God commanded:

> Therefore shall you lay up these my words in your heart and in your soul, and bind them for a sign upon your hand, that they may be as frontlets between your eyes. *And you shall teach them to your children, speaking of them when you sit in your house, and when you walk by the way, when you lie down, and when you rise up. And you shall write them upon the door posts of your house, and upon your gates*: That your days may be multiplied, and the days of your children… [*Deuteronomy 11:18-21 KJV 2000*] Train up a child in the way he should go: and when he is old, he will not depart from it. [*Proverbs 22:6 KJV*]

The Scripture passage requires parents to recognize that education is a high priority, full time, around-the-clock responsibility. The "order from headquarters" come with a promise of a long life for you and for your children. _Consider all of home life to be an educational opportunity for both the children and parents_. Aggressively pursue home schooling or a private faith-based school.

The churches and synagogues must reclaim the responsibility for parental and organized faith-based education. A few hours in a church or synagogue cannot compete with the powerful and compelling influences of continuous immersion in a culture and public government-run schools systems saturated with an aggressively advocated no-god or mini-god, evolution-rooted humanistic worldview. There must be an education alternative.

Home schooling is a great alternative. It is absolutely scriptural and provides parents with the greatest degree of influence and control over the raising of their own children. Home schooled children learn more in 1-2 hours a day than a public school child does in the entire school day. National spelling bees and other similar educational competitions are routinely won or dominated by home schooled children.

The home school resources available today are far superior to the resources available just a few years ago. Active home schooling organizations establish groups for activities such as participation in athletic teams and field trips. Parents and others with special skills draw together small groups of home school children to teach higher level subjects like chemistry, physics, or advanced mathematics. However, many families may not be in a position to engage in home schooling.

Too many churches or synagogues have Monday through Friday pre-school programs allegedly to respond to the needs of changing times. Despite the very best of intentions, preschool programs alone effectively facilitate and even fuel the breakdown of the family. There are many families who are dissatisfied with the public schools and perhaps not equipped for home schooling.

Faith-based schools are no longer just a nice option. They have become vital and essential to the restoration of a passion for freedom and survival of our families and our American culture. Religious and moral teaching feeds the thirst for education and desire to mature in character.

Faith-based schools must become a high priority for parents, but not a substitute for the parents. They must still be consciously involved in the child's education as a way of life. Every moment is a teachable moment; every moment is a role model moment. Educating the children is a continuing around-the-clock responsibility.

Consider just one powerful example—entertainment. *As an expression of God's infinite love*, the Bible prohibits certain prideful, lustful, and immoral thoughts or activities. Such prohibitions are called "sin." Recall that collectively fleeing from all sin is the only way to assure the cohesiveness of the God-designed family—society's most intimate social group—and the sustainability of the freedom-based culture established by God. A stable family and culture is an expression of God's love flowing through us. Interference with that flow ultimately breeds chaos.

Yet, because of America's cultural drift away from God, it became necessary for the movie industry to create the well-known ratings system (G, PG, PG-13, R, and NC-17). Later, the television industry followed (TV-Y, TV-Y7, TVG, TV-PG, TV-14, and TV-MA). The video game industry joined the parade (C, E, E10+, T, M, and AO). If you do not understand the abbreviations, your family is already in deep tapioca.

The inescapable problem with the ratings systems is that they are highly subjective and inevitably decay with time, as formerly forbidden material invades the system. The graded representations of sex (pornography), violence, and profanity become increasingly permissive with each passing year, lowering standards to the point of near nonexistence. Chaos in entertainment is one of the most powerful producers of chaos in the family and the American culture.

Your family is not immune! Each of the three entertainment rating systems is age-related. The assumption is that a maturing individual can tolerate increasing amounts of exposure to uncivil immoral behavior—sin. Whoa! Wait a minute. Why should the Judeo-Christian believer ever tolerate sin? Should we ever accept the premise that viewing or experiencing something is wrong for children or teenagers but acceptable for adults? Sin does not become less serious with age. Of course, physical intimacy becomes acceptable when a man and woman marry, but marriage is not age –dependent.

Remember too that your children will grow up to be just like YOU. If you perceive that it is acceptable to view or experience something clearly expressed in Scripture as offensive go God, your children will do the same, passing on the same perception through at least the third and fourth generations. Elsewhere, it has been demonstrated by one author (Dr. Lloyd Stebbins) that YOU will directly or indirectly influence nearly 2,000,000 people in just four generations. Your personal impact is enormous. You ARE a role model! Be a good one. Select the entertainment for you and your family wisely.

THE PAIN WHEN GOD'S FAMILY TURNS AWAY FROM HIM

History has treated the family as a state within a state attaching to the family a certain "sovereignty." *G.K. Chesterton.* Two people must agree to marriage; only one is necessary to guarantee a government facilitated divorce. Divorce cedes authority to the state, assuring increasing dependence on the state and perpetual domination of the wealthy over the poor and middle class. Consider that most people go to church to be married, but go to the government to be divorced. Marriage costs the state very little, but a huge tax payer-funded bureaucracy is required to support divorce. Many government "entitlement programs" subsidize sin. We pay billions in taxes to support the wrongful choices of others. Marriage preserves freedom from government control. Divorce cedes freedom and control to the government.

Limiting sexual intimacy to the confines of marriage contributes to the permanence of the marriage. True sexual intimacy reflects the intellectual, emotional, and spiritual intimacy (bonding of two souls), which become the mortar that holds together the structure of the marriage. Physical intimacy before marriage allows two people the shallow transient pleasure of a rub and a tickle, rather than unfettered soulful bonding. But that transient experience is so powerful, so all-consuming that it becomes virtually impossible to clearly discern whether or not that partner is the best one to become an irrevocable, lifetime, "til-death-do-us-part" marriage partner. In addition, pornography is so powerful and pervasive that exposure before or after marriage will interfere with godly bonding and the sustainability of the marriage relationship.

Multiple intimate partners, cohabitation, or fornication before marriage weaken or damage the soul and seriously inhibit the ability to make and sustain a lifetime commitment to a marriage partner. Following a series of temporary "bonds," it becomes increasingly difficult to form the pervasive holistic bond that God intended with the one special marriage partner.

Similarly, adultery following the marriage creates the potential for destroying the marriage and family. The devastation painfully damages the spouse, children, siblings of the couple, and many friends. In addition, there is an immediate ripple effect among many people and an extended ripple effect through at least three or four subsequent generations. Is it worth it? Of course not! There is no way that the momentary selfish pleasure even when repeated numerous times can justify the extended sphere of subsequent pain and suffering.

"Let marriage be held in honor among all, and let the marriage bed be undefiled, for *fornicators and adulterers God will judge.*" [*Hebrews 13:4 NAS*] "Thou shalt not commit adultery. Thou shalt not covet." [*Exodus 20:14 & 17 KJV*] Hosea repeatedly forgave his wide Gomer even though she was adulterous and a prostitute. [*Hosea 3:3 KJV*] As always, God's moral law is an expression of His love established for our benefit.

Tasting the original forbidden fruit carried a high price. (1) "When the woman saw that the tree was good for food, and that it was a delight to the eyes, and that the tree was desirable to make one wise, she took from its fruit and ate; and she gave also to her husband with her, and he ate." [*Genesis 3:6 KJV*]. Sin entered the world. Similarly, (2) "The path of the adulteress leads to death." [*Proverbs 2:16-22 KJV*] *"What therefore God hath joined together let not man put asunder." [Matthew 19:6, Mark 10:9 KJV] The command is non-optional and non-negotiable.*

"Lord, grant that I might not so much seek to be loved as to love." *St. Francis of Assisi* "…in everything worth having, even in every pleasure, there is a point of pain or tedium that must be survived, so that the pleasure may be revived and endure." *G.K. Chesterton.*

For troubled Christian marriages, counseling is not likely to be productive unless and until both parties genuinely agree that the Bible is the inspired inerrant word of God and that divorce is NOT an acceptable option outside of serious physical or sexual abuse. The agreed upon mutual view solidifies the common goal to save the marriage. In addition, the husband and wife both have an incentive to resolve troublesome issues because they both desire to enjoy the fullness and richness of the human experience. Since they have both agreed that divorce is unacceptable, the only remaining alternative is to resolve the issues. Often the resolution is facilitated if the effort is framed by the memory of why they originally chose to marry.

LEVERAGE THE FORGOTTEN POWER OF THE HOMEMAKER

Acclaim and demonstrate the vital importance of the homemaker— The Biblical homemaker enjoys the most vital and exciting career in the universe. Family and culture decline rapidly when the homemaker leaves home. To destroy a culture, remove the homemaker from the home. A major strategy of the spiritual and temporal enemies of the traditional family is to deflate or collapse the family by enticing the homemaker out of the home. But God says otherwise, "The women of my people have ye cast out from their pleasant houses; from their children have ye taken away my glory forever. Arise ye, and depart; for this is not your rest: because it is polluted, it shall destroy you, even with a sore destruction." [*Micah 2:9, &10 KJV*] All roads go through the homemaker; she is the real, not just metaphorical heart of the home:

*The homemaker is the heart of the home **physically***—Everyone is born through the womb of the mother. The bond between mother and child begins at the moment of conception and strengthens throughout the child's growing time in the womb as the mother experiences hormonal changes, feels life in the baby's movements, during the actual birth process. No other bond in the universe comes close to matching the early mother-child bond. The bond is reinforced during the period of breast-feeding and continues to grow even as the mother lets go of the emancipated adult. Her loving bond with the father cements the continuity of generations, is a source of personal satisfaction for both, and provides desperately needed role models for the children. Her efforts to maintain or improve the home environment are an expression of love for her husband and children.

*The homemaker is the heart of the home **intellectually***—Scripture assigns parents the responsibility of educating the children. For millennia, the mother was the primary teacher, later assisted by the Church. Schools were created by the Church to teach children about life, God, and His amazing creation. The great universities, including most Ivy League schools, were founded to teach young men to be ministers. But in the last century, the Church and parents have largely abdicated their roles and responsibilities for education in favor of government schools that have become increasingly abusive regarding all aspects of Judeo-Christian tradition. Raising the children is far more than simply taking care of the children.

*The homemaker is the heart of the home **emotionally***—Children learn emotional awareness and compassion far more from the mother than from the father. Indulging a sports analogy, dad is primarily a coach; mom is the quarterback, the source and catalyst of virtually all action in the family and the home. What would happen on game day if the quarterback decided to go fishing instead of instead of going to the stadium? The athletic coach probably has a backup quarterback who may not perform quite as well as the star quarterback. **But in the home, every homemaker is a star and there is no backup when she is not there.**

*The homemaker is the heart of the home **spiritually***—In most homes, it is the mother who primarily instills spiritual principles through day-to-day training. Often it is the mother who takes the children to church or synagogue. Shame on the dads who are not the spiritual leaders in their homes as well. But even in the homes where dad is a strong spiritual leader, the children still spend far more time with the mother and are therefore more available to her for spiritual training. Dad becomes the reinforcer.

These vitally important lessons are not learned when strangers, such as nursery schools, babysitters, an endless round of age-graded day care centers, and government-run schools raise the children. Helicopter and lifestyle absentee parenting is tragic and exposes children to disastrous consequences.

To survive, a family must actively and irrevocably commit to Biblical values and fight aggressively and continuously to maintain those values.

A Homemaker Enjoys the Most Influential and Vital Career in the Universe

A Homemaker enjoys the most influential and vital career in the universe. She is responsible for the stability of a culture and the cohesiveness of the family. She is the panoramic link in time, connecting the generations. She links the past to the future, ancestors to descendants. She is primarily responsible for raising the children in a manner that stabilizes their future and transmits critically important values to the next generation. In short, she makes the home the most desirable place in the universe for her family.

When the homemaker leaves the home, love leaves like air out of a flat tire. The home becomes the house, little more than the building where everyone comes to sleep at night.

Consider the fruit of a family-centered family as opposed to a career-centered family:

- Builds strong cohesive families when Dad is responsible for standard-of-living and Mom is responsible for quality-of-life
- Promotes a partnership between married men and women that grows closer with time

- Children reared by those who love them most... Mom and Dad
- Low risk monogamous sex provides for pleasure and reproduction
- Number and frequency of venereal diseases sharply reduced and largely eliminated
- Few abortions, because the unborn child is an expression of the parents' love
- One man; one woman; one lifetime is the stable marriage norm accepted for six millennia
- Men and women both desire the stability of marriage
- Stable relationships between a man and a woman due to the certainty of the marriage commitment
- Infrequent divorce due to love and respect for spouse as well as responsibility for children
- Legacy of cultural stability passed on to successive generations
- Children experience and enjoy the complementary influences of a mom and a dad
- "Alternative lifestyles" viewed as against nature, culturally destructive, and inappropriate especially when children are involved
- Children are more stable, less stressed, more secure, and behavior is more predictable and...when necessary...more controllable
- Husband and father is vital to the well-being of the family
- Preserves and reinforces the sanctity of life and sanctity of marriage
- Protects and reinforces the sovereignty of the family
- Lifestyle evokes a happier and healthier woman and strong family relationships

What do you think? Have we lost something vitally important in our modern American culture?

Husbands, Would Your Wife Rather Be Home: Encourage Her!

The modern American culture has swerved so far away from the 7-millennium long traditional family-centered culture to the current career-centered culture that young women are virtually forced by cultural pressure to pursue a career as a higher priority than the family. Some have claimed it is possible to have it both ways. The reality is that more and more women are discovering that by definition there can only be one priority. If the priority is career, the family will suffer now and later.

Many women would genuinely prefer to be a homemaker. But those who are brave enough to face the wolfish cultural pressure may be confronted by another barrier closer to home. Today, many married men presumptively expect their wives to have a money-earning job outside the home.

Traditionally—at least up until a few decades ago—men would be embarrassed if their wives worked outside the home. The men were proud of their ability to provide for the material needs and the security of their home. In just a few short decades, their pride succumbed to radical media and feminist pressures and transitioned to, "Honey, it's OK to get a job if you want to; either way is OK with me." The laisse-faire attitude, which was often interpreted by women as uncaring eventually became today's, "Honey, you MUST have a job to help pay all of the bills."

Severe cultural pressures and often poor financial planning create formidable barriers for the would-be homemaker. Here's the rub! Men, if any of you are pressuring your wife to pursue a career, rather than encouraging her to be a homemaker, God has a very direct and stern warning for you. As you read the quote in three translations, remember, "The fear of the Lord is the beginning of wisdom:"

- "The women of my people have ye cast out from their pleasant houses; from their children have ye taken away my glory *forever*. Arise ye, and depart; for this is not your rest: because it is polluted, it shall destroy you, even with a sore destruction." [*Micah 2:9-10 King James Version*]
- "You drive the women of my people from their pleasant homes. You take away my blessing from their children *forever*. Get up, go away! For this is not your resting place, because it is defiled, it is ruined, beyond all remedy." [*Micah 2:9-10 New International Version*]
- "You throw my people's women out of the homes they love. You deprive their children of my glory *forever*. Get up and go! You can't stay here! Because [the land] is now unclean, it will destroy you with a grievous destruction." [*Mikhah 2:9-10 Complete Jewish Bible*]

The clarity of the three scripture translations is inescapable. Regardless of today's cultural pressures, a husband must not encourage his wife to pursue a job outside the home. Whether or not she actually does is another discussion. However, first consider this:

God views the entirety of history as a continuum from Creation through the coming of the Messiah. He sees a holistic master portrait. That portrait includes a seamless parade of generations, each receiving the baton of civilization from the previous generation and passing it on to the next generation. At least that is His intent.

The woman as wife and mother is the link between generations. She learns from the previous generation, primarily from her mother, gives birth to the next generation, and is primarily responsible for nurturing and raising the next generation to become men and women of strong character, capable of carrying the baton of civilization onward to the following generation. *She is ultimately responsible for the cohesiveness of the family and the sustainability of the culture.* She must be praised for her motherhood choice. Of course, when the little one has left the next she can join the workforce and perhaps just continue the part time labor she has engaged in during the child rearing period.

Homemaker "Gap" in Resume

Several years ago, one of the authors (Dr. Lloyd Stebbins) was teaching an MBA course. A woman in the class had devoted a number of years to raising her children who were then grown. At that time, she had other life objectives. That is why she was in the program. During the discussion, she asked me how to handle the "gap" in their resume. I replied that there is no gap. She has served as the:

Chief Operations Officer (COO) of the home, responsible for:

1. *operations and maintenance* of the home,
2. *capital improvements* (remodeling),
3. *purchasing, budgeting, financial management,* and *marketing* (representing the family's interests and reputation inside and outside the home),
4. *managing subcontractors* (plumbers, electricians, appliance repairs, yard workers, etc.),
5. *field operations* (activities related to hobbies, sports, and places of worship),
6. *human resource management* (inspiring and motivating family members to be productive and actively responsible),
7. *personnel training* (raising the children with a strong sense of values), and
8. *environmental management* (greening the home & family worldview).

Building a safe, stress free family organizational culture. Making the home the most desirable place in the universe for the family and raising offspring to become adults of strong character is a boundaryless (24/7) full time responsibility. Serving as a homemaker is much like running a small business. The multidisciplinary wisdom and management experience acquired is applicable to virtually any workplace.

Since then many have benefited from the business language characterization of the responsibilities of the homemaker. As a former business executive, this author would welcome such a description in any resume.

The passage in Micah 2:9 indicates that when the homemaker is "cast out," driven out, or thrown out of the home, to pursue material goals, the missing link forms a disconnect in the flow of generations and the preservation of civilization. The disconnect deprives the children of God's glory for a very long time—the passage says "forever."

Visualize the disconnect as a seamless hand-knit sweater. When a single piece of yarn is broken, a slight tug causes the entire sweater to unravel. Similarly, the entire fabric of America unravels and is rapidly unraveling today when the family link in time is broken. Wow! That's heavy; think about it for a few moments.

The greatest expression of love between a married man and woman is the birth of a child. New parents often cry out, "It's a miracle from God!" and so it is. The child remains every bit as much a miracle at ages 2, 5, 10, 16 or beyond. The miracle child is on loan from God throughout the growing years. God has assigned the enormous responsibility to the parents, primarily the mother, to care for and raise His created miracle to become an adult of strong character who will continue to honor God and pass along an improved baton to the following generation. How could anything be a higher priority?

God places very high and challenging expectations on the woman. Her husband's job is to make her job easy. One day, the parents causing or contributing to a disconnect at the expense of the children will be accountable to God. If that is you, what will you say, when God asks, "What did you do with my miracle?"

NO CIVILIZATION HAS EVER SURVIVED THE BREAKDOWN OF THE FAMILY.

If parents want their children and grandchildren to enjoy a free society (country), they absolutely must deeply embed Biblical family values in their children. ***It is an impossible task for absentee parents.***

It's Shocking That Sin No Longer Shocks!

Sin is still sin. It has not gone away. The overarching message of the Bible from Genesis to Revelation is God's provision for redemption from the ravages of sin. The utter depravity of sin is the baseline from which we are extracted or redeemed, ultimately to experience the fullness of God's love. Yet, today we seldom hear much about sin from the pulpits of America.

The low level of preaching about sin tacitly communicates to believers that sin has a low level of priority or is even unimportant among many Biblical messages. The decades-long decline in the apparent importance of sin encourages believers to flirt with, compromise, or participate in sinful thoughts and activities. The believers' minds rationalize the compromises, in part, by sugar coating their lives with regular attendance at church or synagogue.

Putting distance between us and sin moves us closer to the Lord. While it is important to keep our eye on, "...the goal to win the prize of God's heavenly call in the Messiah Jesus," [*Philippians 3:14 Aramaic Bible in Plain English*] we must be fleeing from sin every moment along the way.

Consider one definition of sin. In its simplest form, sin is just doing things my way instead of God's way. My way is pride-driven, self-indulgent, self-centered and therefore evil, because it is antagonistic to God. God's way is other-centered and an expression of His infinite love. My way and God's way are diametrically opposed and cannot co-exist for very long.

In short, sin is a man or woman's private war with God. It is the equivalent of shaking an angry fist in the face of God, effectively saying, "I don't care what You want; I'm going to do it my way, anyway." Does that form a revolting and unacceptable mental image? Good! Then, we're getting somewhere. Read on.

Sin should always shock, but may not always be surprising. If sin is not shocking, some contemplative self-reflection is in order. We should and must always be shocked by each new disturbing, public revelation about same-sex marriage, pornography, abortion, assisted suicide, cohabitation, divorce, or anything else contrary to the plain reading of scripture.

The recent U.S. Supreme Court ruling on homosexual or lesbian marriage should be a huge shock and wake-up call. Although the decision may not have been surprising in today's culture, a believer must not confuse shock with surprise.

- *Surprise* is emotional. **Shock** is soul-deep
- *Surprise* may provoke anger or joy. **Shock** inspires action, corrective action if sin is involved.
- *Surprise* is temporary. **Shock** is, or should be, enduring.

If you did not understand the difference between surprise and shock, with abundant clarity, before reading this, it may be because many believers (and clergy too) underestimate the depravity of sin, God's utter revulsion of sin, and impact of sin on every area of life.

Light cannot shine in the daytime. It is over taken by the brilliance of the sun. Similarly, the light of the believer cannot shine while basking in the glory of God. He is infinite light. His light overtakes the light of the believer, when he or she is in God's particular presence such as in the protected environment of a place of worship. The light of the believer shines in times and places of spiritual darkness. That is when the believer lights the way for the unbeliever.

The clergy and the body must continually sensitize each other to the evil, disgusting, and relentless nature of sin. We have tended to lose sight of even the definition of sin.

The spirit of believers has become numbed by a secular culture that does not believe the spirit exists. Good preaching lights the way for the believers. But preaching about sin has dwindled in recent decades implying God's approval through the tacit approval of the clergy. Focused, convicting messages have been replaced by feel-good or how-to messages.

A tree can only grow to a height that matches the depth of its root system. Similarly, our sense of the joy of the Lord can only rise to a height that matches the depth of our conviction of sin. Consider the data: After two years of research, George Barna reported:

"What we're finding is that when we ask them (pastors) about all the key issues of the day [90 percent of them are] telling us, 'Yes, the Bible speaks to every one of these issues.' Then we ask them: 'Well, are you teaching your people what the Bible says about those issues?' – and the numbers drop ... to less than 10 percent of pastors who say they will speak to it."

Good heavens! Why not? If the clergy fail to speak forcefully and convincingly to the issues, the people are without direction. The clergy are the ones primarily responsible for applying Biblical truths to today's culture, in an uncompromising way.

Not many decades ago positive cultural and legal pressures encouraged right, moral living. Today, relentless, merciless negative cultural pressures push people nearly irresistibly toward the lures of all manner of sin. The flocks need the collective support of other believers. They also need the strength of their shepherds constantly contrasting the disgusting, evil nature of even so-called minor sins with the glories of God's infinite love and redemption. It is the starkness of the contrast and the enormity of the gap that inspires.

One cannot fully experience the mountain top without knowing the depth of the valleys. *One cannot experience the fullness of God's love without understanding the utter depravity of sin at a soul-deep level*. An intellectual understanding is not sufficient. A transient emotional impression is not sufficient.

It is not necessary to personally experience sin, though to some extent it is driven naturally by the sin nature. Maturity is the lifelong effort to overcome pride and minimize sin in the life of the believer. The Spirit of God will provide conviction through the Bible. The spiritual energy produced must be regularly harnessed and directed by the clergy.

Replace milky messages with meaty ones. "I have fed you with milk, and not with meat: for hitherto ye were not able to bear it..." [*1 Corinthians 3:2 KJV*] Believers are begging for the meat of God's Word. They are ready for it.

Too much preaching today begins at a neutral point, urging people to love God. When neutrality is the starting point there is a reduced perception of a need for God, especially if everything seems to be going well for now. People sense a need for God and experience His love to the extent that they understand the depth and evilness of sin.

God, in His Word, commands us to flee from sin (evil). Various translations of Romans 12:9 order us to:

- Hate evil
- Recoil from what is evil
- Detest evil
- Abhor evil

We can hate, recoil from, detest, or abhor only those things which God hates, recoils from, detests, or abhors, which of course is sin. 1 Corinthians 6:8 requires us to "flee immorality." [*NAS*] 1 Corinthians 10:14 adds the mandate to "flee from idolatry." [*NAS*]

We flee from what we fear. We must fear evil (sin) for its relentless destructive effect on:

- us,
- our interpersonal relationships,
- our children and descendants, and
- our relationship with God.

Unless believers collectively flee from evil, it will destroy our culture and our nation as well.

Sin always separates. Love unites. Sin or evil is the opposite of love. Sin is self-centered and antagonistic to God's nature. Sin cannot coexist with God's love, which is other-centered. "For thou art not a God that hath pleasure in wickedness: neither shall evil dwell with thee. The foolish shall not stand in thy sight: thou hatest all workers of iniquity." [*Psalms 5:4-5 KJV*]

"Let me never forget that the heinousness of sin lies not so much in the nature of the sin committed, as in the greatness of the Person sinned against." [Puritan prayer]

Never Compromise God's Standards

Compromise is the efforts of two people or groups of people sharing common goals and holding plausible but differing views to find and mutually agree upon a common position in between the differing views. However, the Judeo-Christian and Humanist views are directly opposing, irreconcilable, and not amenable to compromise. The Judeo-Christian view is God's perfect standard that He communicated to mankind through Scripture. It is His love letter expressing His infinite love. God's guidelines are often expressed as commands, because breaching those commands triggers certain and often painful results that are inescapably magnified through many other people. Living within His guidelines produces the richest and most satisfying life experience.

Humanism is the complete abandonment of God's standards. Any apparent compromise is simply a partial abandonment of His standards. There cannot be any compromise between God's perfect standards and man's imperfect or flawed standards. For that reason, any attempts to compromise God's standards cannot righteously or logically be either defended or supported. A culture begins to decay when many people begin to compromise ever so slightly, even imperceptibly, in their thoughts, later producing compromise in actions and behaviors. When compromised individual behaviors aggregate in significant numbers, the decay becomes visible across the culture. The visibility reinforces the decay ("everybody's doing it") initiating a slippery downward spiral. When believers compromise in any way, they move toward a godless humanism.

Stop—right now! Imagine the harshest terms you would use to describe life in ancient Sodom and Gomorrah just before God's judgment. Is there any part of that mental image that you could not reasonably apply to America today? What is the difference between what we sense regarding the ancient image compared to the modern one. We are accustomed to thinking of Sodom and Gomorrah in the harshest possible terms, because that is what most of us have been taught. But the same activities today are clothed in the softness of politically correct language. The result is that activities traditionally considered abhorrent are now considered acceptable, desirable, and even worthy of being advocated as good and healthy. In computer terms, the activities viewed as sins for 6,000 years have become "user friendly." Did that illustration grab your attention? Did today's cultural decay seem to sneak up on you? Are YOU sufficiently disturbed to want to do something about it?

An enormous personal responsibility is attached to each of God's guidelines, especially when they are expressed as commands. Any time YOU—or this writer, for that matter—chooses to deviate even minimally from God's specific directions, it is the equivalent of looking directly at God, shaking a fist at Him, and exclaiming, "God, I don't care what you want, I'm going to do what I want." *It is your own personal war with God.* Does that evoke a revolting, totally unacceptable mental image? Good! We have made considerable progress.

While tending the flocks of his father-in-law, God appeared to Moses through a burning bush. "God called to him out of the midst of the bush." [*Exodus 3:4 KJV*] After receiving God's message, Moses asks God for His name. God replied, "I AM THAT I AM." [*Exodus 3:14 KJV*] It may seem like an odd way for God to refer to Himself—perhaps a bit difficult to understand. But God clarifies His statement in the Ten Commandments, "Thou shalt have no other gods before me." [*Exodus 20:3 KJV*] and again "I am the Lord, and there is no other; apart from Me there is no God. [*Isaiah 45:5 NIV*]

The God-designed Family Is Impregnable

Through Isaiah, God recognized the inevitable result when people abandon Him. "YOU trusted in your wickedness: Your wisdom and knowledge mislead YOU; when you say to yourself, *I am and there is none besides me.*" [*Isaiah 47:10 NIV*] At that point, man has become his own "I am;" Man has become his own god. God has clearly and forcefully condemned humanism thousands of years before the word "humanism" was invented. There follows a fearful price to be paid by any individual or any culture that abandons God, "Disaster will come upon you, and you will not know how to conjure it away. A calamity will fall upon you that you cannot ward off with a ransom; a catastrophe you cannot foresee will suddenly come upon you. [*Isaiah 47:11 NIV*]

Jehovah is the one and only God and will not accept any distractions or priorities that would in any way weaken His relationship with anyone. Virtually all people of Judeo-Christian tradition have heard messages indicating that a god need not be an imagined deity or a statue. Anything such as materialism, alcohol, or even golf that dominates a person's life, to the extent of jeopardizing relationships with God, family, or others can and will become a god.

Evolution-driven humanism is the extreme where man becomes his own god. A powerful scriptural warning is provided in Isaiah. In that passage, God declares the wickedness of the man who says, "I am and there is no other." Anyone who claims to be, "I am" has replaced and abandoned the "I AM" of God. The scriptural consequence that follows is not pretty. Very few people on extremely rare occasions would ever stand up in front of a group of others claiming, "I am god." But people effectively do the same thing each time they choose to do something their way instead of God's way. They are in effect saying, "I am the god of _____ (fill in the blank with any of the selfish choices YOU (Insert Image_13 to right of text)have made in this lifetime). As the selfish choices accumulate in the life of any one person, the ultimate aggregate result is that the person becomes his own god, whether or not the claim is ever verbalized.

On February 3, 1943, the U.S.A.T. (United States Army Transport) *Dorchester* was carrying troops to Europe. Just after midnight, the *Dorchester* was torpedoed by a German submarine in the frigid waters near Greenland. In less than twenty minutes, the ship disappeared beneath those waters, taking along with it four extraordinary chaplains, including Rabbi Alexander Goode (Jewish), Reverend Clark Poling (Dutch Reform), Reverend George Fox (Methodist), and Father John Washington (Catholic). All four held the military rank of Lieutenant. Throughout the chaotic and terrifying twenty minutes amidst the terrifying cries of the wounded and frightened, the four chaplains took over, calming the crowd of soldiers. The chaplains guided the men towards safety, passed out life jackets, and help others climb into life boats. When no more life jackets remained, all four chaplains took off theirs insisting that other soldiers wear them. Later, survivors testified that as the ship was submerging, the four chaplains stood on the deck with their arms interlocked as they sang and prayed together; the rabbi sang and prayed in Hebrew, the priest in Latin, and the ministers in English. Just 230 of the 902 men on board survived. The four chaplains, a Jew, a Methodist, Dutch Reform, and a Catholic willingly gave their lives that others may live. One of the survivors exclaimed, "It was the finest thing I have ever seen this side of heaven." "Greater love hath no man than this, that a man lay down his life for his friends."[6] [*John 15:15 KJV*]

In perilous times, there will be people "Having a form of godliness, but denying the power thereof…Ever learning, and never able to come to the knowledge of the truth." [*2 Timothy 3: 5 & 7 KJV*] Never be satisfied with a "form of godliness." Do everything God's way. You will be glad you did.

CHAPTER 9 NOTES

1. Bishop Samuel Fallows, Introduction to T. W. Shannon, *Eugenics or The Laws of Sex Life and Heredity* (Garden City, New York: Doubleday & Company, 1970, replica edition of Marietta, Ohio: S. A. Mullikin Company, 1917) 9

2. T. W. Shannon, *Eugenics or The Laws of Sex Life and Heredity* (Garden City, New York: Doubleday & Company, 1970, replica edition of Marietta, Ohio: S. A. Mullikin Company, 1917) 32.

3. Ibid. 35.

4. G.K. Chesterton, *Collected Works, Volume IV: What's Wrong with the World; The Superstition of Divorce; Eugenics and Other Evils*, (San Francisco: Ignatius Press, 1987), p. 254.

5. Ibid. p. 442.

6. Wallbuilders, The Four Chaplains, http://www.wallbuilders.com/LIBissuesArticles.asp?id=151956

ABOUT THE AUTHORS

JUDITH REISMAN, PH.D.

As a researcher & author, historian & teacher, Judith Reisman has focused on pornography as a pandemic, addicting men, women and children and upon exposing Dr. Alfred C. Kinsey's fraudulent sex science research and education.

Current occupations:

- Professor of Psychology, Liberty University School of Behavioral Sciences
- Director, The Reisman Institute, FKA, The Child Protection Institute
- Scientific Adviser, California Protective Parents Association
- Distinguished Senior Fellow, The Inter-American Institute
- President, Institute for Media Education

An eager news and media analyst, she writes for Salvo Magazine, WorldNetDaily and was principal investigator for the pioneering U.S. Department of Justice, Juvenile Justice study *Images of Children, Crime and Violence in Playboy, Penthouse and Hustler*. She authored *Kinsey, Sex and Fraud, Soft Porn Plays Hardball, Partner Solicitation Language as a Reflection of Male Sexual Orientation, Kinsey, Crimes & Consequences* and *Sexual*

<u>Sabotage</u>. In 2013, Liberty Counsel republished *Kinsey: Crimes & Consequences'* 4th edition as <u>Stolen Honor Stolen Innocence</u>.

As scientific consultant to four U.S. Department of Justice administrations, the U.S. Department of Education, and the U.S. Department of Health and Human Services, she is listed in *Who's Who in Science & Engineering, International Who's Who in Sexology, International Who's Who in Education, Who's Who of American Women, The World's Who's Who of Women*, etc. Based on her work, *The German Medical Tribune* and the British medical journal, *The Lancet* demanded that the Kinsey Institute be investigated for deliberately covering up massive sex crimes against children and fraudulent science.

About The Authors

LLOYD H. STEBBINS, PH.D.

Dr. Lloyd H. Stebbins has been on a personal journey for about fifteen years, during which he experienced the convergence of several factors in his personal and professional life. Personally, he cared for his late wife around the clock for seven years. She suffered from a chronic neurodegenerative conditions similar to Alzheimer's disease that eventually cost her life. Despite the obvious tragedy and personal challenges, it was a monumentally life changing experience for him. Throughout tough times, when others often turned their backs, the Lord's presence was as real to the author as another person sharing the same sofa. The emotional and spiritual rewards evoked by taking care of a loved one too disabled to communicate any form of appreciation are so great as to defy description and are largely unknown in modern self-absorbed American culture.

That intense personal experience and others along with personal observations triggered the emergence of a heart wrenching concern for the fall of the family and the collapse of the American culture. The decades-long observations and concerns crescendoed in recent years. The path to family and cultural decay is traced and detailed in his book, *Life, Liberty, and the Pursuit of Happiness: YOU Must Save America and the Family*. However, unlike other books, this focused history lesson spans just the first few chapters. The ten remaining chapters develop the "Awesome Remedy."

Earning dual academic qualifications in both the natural sciences, including chemical engineering, and business management enabled Dr. Stebbins to fully appreciate the spectacular successes of the scientific method of investigation and also to question its blind application to the social sciences. From its earliest beginnings, the public fascination with the scientific method spread rapidly throughout all western civilization and eventually dominated virtually all ordinary thought and behavior, albeit without the fancy scientific terminology. Today, science has become a faith, at least outside of the scientific world, which demands nearly absolute obedience. Such obedience comes at a very high social cost that leads to questioning the modern definition of *science* and subsequently shining a bright light on a refreshing earlier view of science that held until the last century and a half.

The dovetailing personal and professional experiences evoked a growing awareness that Judeo-Christian culture has drifted away from God in recent decades just a few steps behind the drift of the background secular culture. The ultimate inescapable conclusion is that virtually all modern social controversies are rooted in that drift. The resolution of the controversies is rooted in reversing the drift at least among Judeo-Christian believers and recapturing the real meaning of freedom which is a gift from the Creator, not from government.

Dr. Stebbins currently serves several universities as an adjunct professor teaching both natural science and business management courses. He can be reached at lsteb@brighthouse.com.

Dr. Stebbins publishing experience includes a doctoral dissertation and hundreds of articles for periodicals.

THE MOST IMPORTANT CHALLENGE OF YOUR LIFE!

Dr. Alfred Kinsey's primary mission was to fundamentally transform the American culture to accommodate all manner of moral perversion, sexual excesses, and behaviors considered deviant by most of the world throughout virtually all of civilized history. His strategy stemmed from his virulent hostility toward the Bible, Judeo-Christian believers, and anything that smacks of religion. Kinsey and his cadre of highly influential supporters in the Rockefeller foundation, the American Civil Liberties Union (ACLU), Planned Parenthood (PP), American Bar Association (ABA), and even justices on the United States Supreme Court revised the American Law Institute-Model Penal Code.

Kinsey's lawyer and friend Morris Ernst served as a personal representative for President Roosevelt during World War II and a founding member of the ACLU. Ernst was also the attorney for Kinsey, Margaret Sanger [founder of PP], the Kinsey Institute, the Sex Information and Education Council of the United States (SIECUS), and Planned Parenthood of America. These organizations are the sources of most of the so-called sex education materials saturating the United States public school systems, kindergarten through 12th grade. Further, Ernst maintained close ties with progressive Unites States Supreme Court Justices Louis Brandeis, Brennon, Frankfurter and also Judge Learned Hand, Chief Judge and Senior Judge of the U. S. Circuit Court of appeals for the Second Circuit.

In 1948, Morris Ernst and his associate David Loth targeted 52 sex crimes for abolition or "lightening." Most paralleled Biblical prohibitions, which had stabilized the cultures of the American colonies and the subsequent United States culture for nearly 400 years. Today, most of the targeted laws have been repealed, unleashing the cultural chaos evident to any observer.

By 1989, the National Research Council split contemporary American history into the "pre and post Kinsey eras." Today, virtually all forms of "recreational sex" have been legalized. The only remaining legal test is "consent." Legalization of underlying bad behavior serves to enable and progressively promote even more extreme abuses.

Although Dr. Kinsey died in 1956, his legacy has been amplified and continues to have a major impact. The Kinsey Institute still exists and operates at Indiana University. The Institute and its progeny are the sources of much of the so-called sex education material plaguing the public schools. Kinsey and his work continues to be cited in legal cases and in scholarly journals in the fields of law, psychology, and sociology. The Kinsey scale purports to put heterosexuality and homosexuality on a spectrum or sliding scale from 100% heterosexual to 100% homosexual. It has become the basis for the perverted notion of gender fluidity promoted so often in contemporary media.

Endorsement by academia formally passes moral and ethical abuses to the next generation. Each succeeding generation moves the bar of acceptable behavior to a lower level, relentlessly marching toward inevitable cultural chaos.

Kinsey's legacy continues to be promoted by the ACLU and Planned Parenthood and even—albeit unknowingly—in ordinary conversations among people who have never heard of Kinsey.

By intent, propelled by Kinsey's cadre and many others, the traditional Biblical family has been dangerously destabilized and the definition of the family has been tragically diffused to include virtually any bizarre or fanciful group of consenting individuals.

Nevertheless, the family has been the main source of stability of every civilization that has existed since the days of the ancient Israelites. The destabilization of the family has always resulted in civilizational collapse. Why? Quite simply the family is the basic building block of all societies. The family is the cultural anchor.

Judeo-Christian families have an even deeper and far stronger anchor. He is God, clearly known through his personal love letter, the Holy Bible. His extended letter expressed as a book proclaims that ***the ONLY way a stable culture can be passed on from generation to generation and on to posterity is through the Biblical virtues and values transmitted by strong, loving, families.***

Virtually all Scriptural mandates and prohibitions are directly or indirectly intended to preserve the sanctities of life, marriage, and family. Consider the Ten Commandments as one of many examples. They are often taught as two groups. The first four govern the vertical relationship between an individual and God; the last six govern the horizontal relationships among an individual, spouse, family members and all others. Yet, the first four establish God's priority and are prerequisites for successfully living the last six. Hence, all are required to assure the sanctities of life, marriage, and family.

Ultimately, Jonah had no choice but to proclaim God's message to the wicked at Nineveh. Today, as America declines, the traditional Biblical family continues to fracture and scatter. America is rapidly becoming (or perhaps already has become) a modern day Nineveh. What now? Like Jonah, God is calling us to "Arise and go to [our own] Nineveh. The authors along with all committed Judeo-Christian believers reading this book no longer have a choice. They (we) MUST go to the American Nineveh, rescue the disintegrating family and proclaim God's loving Word loudly, clearly, consistently, and urgently. To be creditable, we must build God's message into our own lives in a way that is clearly visible, convincing, and enviable.

You cannot unread this book.

From here on, the rest is up to YOU.

THAT IS YOUR GREATEST CHALLENGE!

CPSIA information can be obtained
at www.ICGtesting.com
Printed in the USA
LVHW050205210722
723935LV00008B/273